Diary of
ANNA GREEN WINSLOW

A BOSTON SCHOOL GIRL OF 1771

WITH AN INTRODUCTION AND NOTES
BY
ALICE MORSE EARLE

APPLEWOOD BOOKS
Bedford, Massachusetts

Diary of Anna Green Winslow was originally published in 1894 by Houghton & Mifflin of Boston.

ISBN 1-55709-447-0

Thank you for purchasing an Applewood Book. Applewood reprints America's lively classics—books from the past that are of interest to modern readers. For a free copy of our current catalog, write to: Applewood Books, P.O. Box 365, Bedford, MA 01730.

10 9 8 7 6 5 4 3 2 1

Printed in the United States of America.

Library of Congress Cataloging-in-Publication Data
Winslow, Anna Green, 1759–1779.
    Diary of Anna Green Winslow: a Boston school girl of 1771 / edited by Alice Morse Earle.
        p.   cm.
    Originally published: Boston: Houghton & Mifflin, 1894.
    ISBN 1-55709-447-0
    1. Boston (Mass.)—Social life and customs—Juvenile literature.   2. Boston (Mass.)—History—Colonial period, ca. 1600–1775—Juvenile literature.   3. Winslow, Anna Green, 1759–1779—Diaries—Juvenile literature.
 4. Girls—Massachusetts—Boston—Diaries—Juvenile literature.   I. Earle, Alice Morse, 1851–1911.   II. Title.
F73.4.W78   1996
974.4'6102'092–dc20
[B]   96-9810
                                                            CIP

This Book

IS DEDICATED
TO
THE KINSFOLK OF

ANNA GREEN WINSLOW

FOREWORD.

*I*N the year 1770, a bright little girl ten
years of age, Anna Green Winslow, was
sent from her far away home in Nova Scotia
to Boston, the birthplace of her parents, to
be "finished" at Boston schools by Boston
teachers. She wrote, with evident eagerness
and loving care, for the edification of her parents and her own practice in penmanship, this
interesting and quaint diary, which forms
a most sprightly record, not only of the life
of a young girl at that time, but of the prim
and narrow round of daily occurrences in provincial Boston. It thus assumes a positive
value as an historical picture of the domestic
life of that day ; a value of which the little
girl who wrote it, or her kinsfolk who affec-
tionately preserved it to our own day, never
could have dreamed. To many New England families it is specially interesting as a
complete rendering, a perfect presentment, of
the childish life of their great grandmothers,
her companions.

It is an even chance which ruling thought
in

in the clever little writer, a love of religion or a love of dress, shows most plainly its influence on this diary. On the whole, I think that youthful vanity, albeit of a very natural and innocent sort, is more pervasive of the pages. And it is fortunate that this is the case; for, from the frankly frivolous though far from self-conscious entries we gain a very exact notion, a very valuable picture, of the dress of a young girl at that day. We know all the details of her toilet, from the "pompedore" shoes and the shifts (which she had never worn till she lived in Boston), to the absurd and top-heavy head-decoration of "black feathers, my past comb & all my past garnet marquasett and jet pins, together with my silver plume." If this fantastic assemblage of ornament were set upon the "Heddus roll," so graphically described, it is easy to understand the denunciations of the time upon women's headgear. In no contemporary record or account, no matter who the writer, can be found such a vivacious and witty description of the modish hairdressing of that day as in the pages of this diary.

But there are many entries in the journal of this vain little Puritan devotee to show an almost equal attention to religion; records of sermons which she had heard, and of religious

gious conversations in which she had taken a
self-possessed part; and her frequent use of
Biblical expressions and comparisons shows
that she also remembered fully what she
read. Her ambitious theological sermon-notes
were evidently somewhat curtailed by the sensible advice of the aunt with whom she resided,
who thereby checked also the consequent inju-
dicious praise of her pastor, the Old South
minister. For Anna and her kinsfolk were
of the congregation of the Old South church;
and this diary is in effect a record of the life
of Old South church attendants. Many were
what Anna terms "sisters of the Old South,"
and nine tenths of the names of her companions and friends may be found on the baptismal and membership records of that church.

Anna was an industrious little wight, active
in all housewifely labors and domestic accomplishments, and attentive to her lessons. She
could make "pyes," and fine network; she
could knit lace, and spin linen thread and
woolen yarn; she could make purses, and em-
broider pocket-books, and weave watch strings,
and piece patchwork. She learned " dansing,
or danceing I should say," from one Master
Turner; she attended a sewing school, to become a neat and deft little sempstress, and
above all, she attended a writing school to
                                        learn

learn that most indispensable and most appreciated of eighteenth century accomplishments — fine writing. Her handwriting, of which a fac-simile is here shown, was far better than that of most girls of twelve to-day ; with truth and justice could Anna say, " Aunt says I can write pretily." Her orthography was quite equal to that of grown persons of her time, and her English as good as that of Mercy Warren, her older contemporary writer.

And let me speak also of the condition of her diary. It covers seventy-two pages of paper about eight inches long by six and a half inches wide. The writing is uniform in size, every letter is perfectly formed ; it is as legible as print, and in the entire diary but three blots can be seen, and these are very small. A few pages were ruled by the writer, the others are unruled. The old paper, though heavy and good, is yellow with age, and the water marks C. J. R. and the crown stand out distinctly. The sheets are sewed in a little book, on which a marbled paper cover has been placed, probably by a later hand than Anna's. Altogether it is a remarkably creditable production for a girl of twelve.

It is well also to compare her constant diligence and industry displayed to us through her records of a day's work — and at another
time,

*time, of a week's work — with that of any
girl of her age in a corresponding station of
life nowadays. We learn that physical pain
or disability were no excuse for slothfulness;
Anna was not always well — had heavy colds,
and was feverish; but well or ill was always
employed. Even with painful local afflictions
such as a "whitloe," she still was industrious,
"improving it to perfect myself in learning to
spin flax." She read much — the Bible constantly — and also found amusement in reading "a variety of composures."*

*She was a friendly little soul, eager to be
loved; resenting deeply that her Aunt Storer
let "either one of her chaises, her chariot or
babyhutt," pass the door every day, without
sending for her; going cheerfully tea-drinking
from house to house of her friends; delight-
ing even in the catechising and the sober Thursday Lecture. She had few amusements and
holidays compared with the manifold pleas-
ures that children have nowadays, though she
had one holiday which the Revolution struck
from our calendar — the King's Coronation
Day. She saw the Artillery Company drill,
and she visited brides and babies and old
folks, and attended some funerals. When
she was twelve years old she "came out" —
became a "miss in her teens" — and went to a
succession*

*succession of prim little routs or parties,
which she called "constitutions." To these
decorous assemblies girls only were invited,
— no rough Boston boys. She has left to us
more than one clear, perfect picture of these
formal little routs in the great low-raftered
chamber, softly alight with candles on mantel-
tree and in sconces; with Lucinda, the black
maid, "shrilly piping;" and rows of demure
little girls of Boston Brahmin blood, in high
rolls and feathers, discreetly partaking of hot
and cold punch, and soberly walking and curtsy-
ing through the minuet; fantastic in costume,
but proper and seemly in demeanor, models of
correct deportment as were their elegant mam-
mas.*

*But Anna was not solemn; she was always
happy, and often merry — full of life and
wit. She jested about getting a "fresh seasoning with Globe salt," and wrote some
labored jokes and some unconscious ones home
to her mother. She was subject to "egregious
fits of laughterre," and fully proved the state-
ment, "Aunt says I am a whimsical child."
She was not beautiful. Her miniature is
now owned by Miss Elizabeth C. Trott of
Niagara Falls, the great grand-daughter of
General John Winslow, and a copy is shown
in the frontispiece. It displays a gentle, win-
ning*

ning little face, delicate in outline, as is also the figure, and showing some hint also of delicacy of constitution. It may be imagination to think that it is plainly the face of one who could never live to be old — a face typical of youth.

*L*ET us glance at the stock from whence sprung this tender and engaging little blossom. When the weary Pilgrims landed at Cape Cod before they made their memorable landing at Plymouth, a sprightly young girl jumped on shore, and was the first English woman to set foot on the soil of New England. Her name was Mary Chilton. She married John Winslow, the brother of Governor Edward Winslow. Anna Green Winslow was Mary Chilton's direct descendant in the sixth generation.

Anna's grandfather, John Winslow the fourth, was born in Boston. His son Joshua wrote thus in the Winslow Family Bible: "Jno Winslow my Honor'd Father was born ye 31 Dec. at 6 o'c. in the morning on the Lords Day, 1693, and was baptized by Mr. Willard the next day & dyed att sea Octo. 13, 1731 aged 38 years." A curious attitude was assumed by certain Puritan ministers, of reluctance

*luctance and even decided objection and re-
fusal to baptize children who were unlucky
enough to be born on the Lord's Day ; but
Samuel Willard, the pastor of the "South
Church" evidently did not concur in that extraordinary notion, for on the day following
"Jno's" birth — on New Year's Day — he was
baptized.   He was married on September 21,
1721, to Sarah Pierce, and in their ten years
of married life they had three children.*

*Joshua Winslow, Anna's father, was the
second child.   He was born January 23, 1727,
and was baptized at the Old South.   He was
"published" with his cousin Anna Green on
December 7, 1758, and married to her four
weeks later, January 3, 1759.   An old piece
of embroidered tapestry herein shown gives a
good portrayal of a Boston wedding-party at
that date ; the costumes, coach, and cut of the
horses' mane and tail are very curious and
interesting to note.   Mrs. Winslow's mother
was Anna Pierce (sister of Sarah), and her
father was Joseph Green, the fourth generation from Percival Green, whose descendants
have been enumerated by Dr. Samuel Abbott
Green, the president of the Massachusetts Historical Society, in his book entitled "Account
of Percival and Ellen Green and some of their
descendants."*

Mrs.

Mrs. Joshua Winslow was the oldest of twelve Green children, hence the vast array of uncles and aunts and cousins in little Anna's diary.

Joseph Green, Anna's maternal grandfather, was born December 12, 1703, and was baptized on the same day. He died July 11, 1765. He was a wealthy man for his time, being able to pay Governor Belcher £ 3,600 for a tract of land on Hanover Street. His firm name was Green & Walker. A fine portrait of him by Copley still exists.

Thus Anna came of good stock in all lines of descent. The Pierces were of the New Hampshire provincial gentry, to which the Wentworths and Langdons also belonged.

Before Joshua Winslow was married, when he was but eighteen years of age, he began his soldierly career. He was a Lieutenant in Captain Light's company in the regiment of Colonel Moore at the taking of Louisburg in 1745. He was then appointed Commissary-General of the British forces in Nova Scotia, and an account-book of his daily movements there still exists. Upon his return to New England he went to live at Marshfield, Massachusetts, in the house afterwards occupied by Daniel Webster. But troublous times were now approaching for the faithful servants of the

the King.   Strange notions of liberty filled
the heads of many Massachusetts men and
women; and soon the Revolution became more
than a dream.   Joshua Winslow in that cri-
sis, with many of his Marshfield friends and
neighbors, sided with his King.

He was in Marshfield certainly in June,
1775, for I have a letter before me written
to him there by Mrs. Deming at that date.
One clause of this letter is so amusing that I
cannot resist quoting it.   We must remember
that it was written in Connecticut, whence
Mrs. Deming had fled in fright and dismay
at the siege of Boston ; and that she had lost
her home and all her possessions.   She writes
in answer to her brother's urgent invitation to
return to Marshfield.

"We have no household stuff.   Neither
could I live in the terror of constant alarms
and the din of war.   Besides I know not how
to look you in the face, unless I could restore
to you your family Expositer, which together
with my Henry on the Bible & Harveys
Meditations which are your daughter's (the
gift of her grandmother) I pack'd in a Trunk
that exactly held them, some days before I
made my escape, and did my utmost to git
to you, but which I am told are still in Boston.   It is not, nor ever will be in my power

to

to make you Satisfaction for this Error — I should not have coveted to keep 'em so long — I am heartily sorry now that I had more than one book at a time ; in that case I might have thot to have bro't it away with me, tho' I forgot my own Bible & almost every other necessary. But who can tell whether you may not git your Valuable Books. I should feel comparatively easy if you had these your Valuable property."

Her painful solicitude over the loss of a borrowed book is indeed refreshing, as well as her surprising covetousness of the Family Expositor and Harvey's Meditations. And I wish to add to the posthumous rehabilitation of the damaged credit of this conscientious aunt, that Anna's book — Harvey's Meditations — was recovered and restored to the owner, and was lost at sea in 1840 by another Winslow.

Joshua Winslow, when exiled, went to England, and thence to Quebec, where he retained throughout his life his office as Royal Paymaster. He was separated many years from his wife and daughter, and doubtless Anna died while her father was far from her ; for in a letter dated Quebec, December 26, 1783, and written to his wife, he says,

" *The*

" *The Visiting Season is come on, a great practice here about Christmas and the New Year; on the return of which I congratulate my Dearest Anna and Friends with you, it being the fifth and I hope the last I shall be obliged to see the return of in a Separation from each other while we may continue upon the same Globe.*"

She shortly after joined him in Quebec. His letters show careful preparations for her comfort on the voyage. They then were childless; Anna's brothers, George Scott and John Henry, died in early youth. It is interesting to note that Joshua Winslow was the first of the Winslows to give his children more than one baptismal name.

Joshua Winslow was a man of much dignity and of handsome person, if we can trust the Copley portrait and miniature of him which still exist. The portrait is owned by Mr. James F. Trott of Niagara Falls, New York, the miniature by Mrs. J. F. Lindsey of Yorkville, South Carolina, both grandchildren of General John Winslow. His letters display much intelligence. His spelling is unusually correct; his penmanship elegant — as was that of all the Winslows; his forms of expression scholarly and careful. He sometimes

times could joke a little, as when he began his letters to his wife Anna thus — 2. N. A. — though it is possible that the " Obstructions to a free Correspondence, and the Circumspection we are obliged to practice in our Converse with each other" arising from his exiled condition, may have made him thus use a rebus in the address of his letter.

He died in Quebec in 1801. His wife returned to New England and died in Medford in 1816. Her funeral was at General John Winslow's house on Purchase Street, Fort Hill, Boston ; she was buried in the Winslow tomb in King's Chapel burial ground.

*W*E know little of the last years of Anna Green Winslow's life. A journal written by her mother in 1773 during their life in Marshfield is now owned by Miss Sarah Thomas of Marshfield, Mass. It is filled chiefly with pious sermon notes and religious thoughts, and sad and anxious reflections over absent loved ones, one of whom (in the sentimental fashion of the times) she calls " my Myron" — her husband.*

Through this journal we see " Nanny Green's" simple and monotonous daily life ; her little tea-drinkings ; her spinning and reeling

reeling and knitting; her frequent catechisings, her country walks. We find her mother's testimony to the " appearance of reason that is in my children and for the readiness with which they seem to learn what is taught them." And though she repeatedly thanks God for living in a warm house, she notes that " my bason of water froze on the hearth with as good a fire as we could make in the chimney." This rigor of climate and discomfort of residence, and Anna's evident delicacy shown through the records of her fainting, account for her failing health. The last definite glimpse which we have of our gentle little Nanny is in the shape of a letter written to her by "Aunt Deming." It is dated Boston, April 21, 1779, and is so characteristic of the day and so amusing also that I quote it in full.

    Dear Neice,

                I receivd your favor of 6th instant by nephew Jack, who with the Col. his trav'ling companion, perform'd an easy journey from you to us, and arriv'd before sunset. I thank you for the beads, the wire, and the beugles, I fancy I shall never execute the plan of the head dress to which you allude — if I should, some of your largest corn stalks,

stalks, dril'd of the pith and painted might be more proportionable. I rejoice that your cloths came off so much better than my fears — a troublesome journey, I expected you would have; and very much did I fear for your bones. I was always unhappy in anticipating trouble — it is my constitution, I believe — and when matters have been better than my fears — I have never been so dutifully thankful as my bountiful Benefactor had a right to expect. This, also, I believe, is the constitution of all my fellow race.

Mr. Deming had a Letter from your Papa yesterday; he mention'd your Mama & you as indispos'd & Flavia as sick in bed. I'm at too great a distance to render you the least service, and were I near, too much out of health to — some part of the time — even speak to you. I am seiz'd with exceeding weakness at the very seat of life, and to a greater degree than I ever before knew. Could I ride, it might help me, but that is an exercise my income will not permit. I walk out whenever I can. The day will surely come, when I must quit this frail tabernacle, and it may be soon — I certainly know, I am not of importance eno' in this world, for any one to wish my stay — rather am I, and so I consider myself as a cumberground. However

I

I shall abide my appointed time & I desire to be found waiting for my change.

Our family are well — had I time and spirits I could acquaint you of an expedition two sisters made to Dorchester, a walk begun at sunrise last thursday morning — dress'd in their dammasks, padusoy, gauze, ribbins, flapets, flowers, new white hats, white shades, and black leather shoes, (Pudingtons make) and finished journey, & garments, orniments, and all quite finish'd on Saturday, before noon, (mud over shoes) never did I behold such destruction in so short a space — bottom of padusoy coat fring'd quite round, besides places worn entire to floss, & besides frays, dammask, from shoulders to bottom, not lightly soil'd, but as if every part had rub'd tables and chairs that had long been us'd to wax mingl'd with grease. I could have cry'd, for I really pitied'em — nothing left fit to be seen — They had leave to go, but it never entered any ones tho'ts but their own to be dressd in all (even to loading) of their best — their all, as you know. What signifies it to worry ones selves about beings that are, and will be, just so? I can, and do pity and advise, but I shall git no credit by such like. The eldest talks much of learning dancing, musick (the spinet & guitar), embroidry, dresden, the
French

French tongue &c &c. The younger with an air of her own, advis'd the elder when she first mention'd French, to learn first to read English, and was answered " law, so I can well eno' a'ready." You've heard her do what she calls reading, I believe. Poor creature! Well! we have a time of it!

If any one at Marshfield speaks of me remember me to them. Nobody knows I'm writing, each being gone their different ways, & all from home except the little one who is above stairs. Farewell my dear, I've wrote eno' I find for this siting.

Yr affect

Sarah Deming.

It does not need great acuteness to read between the lines of this letter an affectionate desire to amuse a delicate girl whom the writer loved. The tradition in the Winslow family is that Anna Green Winslow died of consumption at Marshfield in the fall of 1779. There is no town or church record of her death, no known grave or headstone to mark her last resting-place. And to us she is not dead, but lives and speaks — always a loving, endearing little child; not so passionate and gifted and rare a creature as that star among children — Marjorie Fleming — but a natural and

*and homely little flower of New England life;
fated never to grow old or feeble or dull or
sad, but to live forever and laugh in the gla-
mour of eternal happy youth through the few
pages of her time-stained diary.*

Alice Morse Earle.

Brooklyn Heights, September, 1894.

LIST OF ILLUSTRATIONS.

PAGE

ANNA GREEN WINSLOW. From miniature now owned
by Miss Elizabeth C. Trott, Niagara Falls, N. Y.
Frontispiece.

FACSIMILE OF WRITING OF ANNA GREEN WINSLOW.
From original diary   1

WEDDING PARTY IN BOSTON IN 1756. From tapestry
now owned by American Antiquarian Society . . . 20

GENERAL JOSHUA WINSLOW. From miniature painted
by Copley, 1755, and now owned by Mrs. John F.
Lindsey, Yorkville, S. C. 34

EBENEZER STORER. From portrait painted by Copley,
now owned by Mrs. Lewis C. Popham, Scarsdale,
N. Y. 45

HANNAH GREEN STORER. From portrait painted by
Copley, now owned by Mrs. Lewis C. Popham, Scarsdale, N. Y. 65

CUT-PAPER PICTURE. Cut by Mrs. Sarah Winslow
Deming, now owned by James F. Trott, Esq., Niagara Falls, N. Y. 74

I hope aunt wont let me wear the black hatt with the red Dominie — for the people will ask me what I have got to sell as I go along street if I do. or, how the folk at Newguinie do? Dear mamma, you dont know the fation here — I beg to look like other folk. You dont kno what a stir would be made in sudbury street were I to make my appearance there in my red Domine & black Hatt. But the old cloak & bonnett together will make me a decent Bonnet for common ocation (I like that aunt says, its a pitty some of the ribbin you sent wont do for the Bonnet — I must now close up this Journal. With Duty, Love, & Compliments as due. perticularly to my Dear little brother, (I long to se him) & Mrs Law, I will write to her soon I am Honrd Popa & mama,

Yr ever Dutiful Daughter

Anna Green Winslow.

N. B. my aunt Deming, dont approve of my English. It has not the fear that you will think her concernd in the
Dutton

DIARY OF ANNA GREEN WINSLOW.

1771–1773.

.   .   .   .

Lady, by which means I had a bit of the wedding cake. I guess I shall have but little time for journalising till after thanksgiving. My aunt Deming[1] says I shall make one pye myself at least. I hope somebody beside myself will like to eat a bit of my Boston pye thou' my papa and you did not (I remember) chuse to partake of my Cumberland[2] performance. I think I have been writing my own Praises this morning. Poor Job was forced to praise himself when no *man* would do him that justice. I am not as he was. I have made two shirts for unkle since I finish'd mamma's shifts.

Novr 18th, 1771. — Mr. Beacons[3] text yesterday was Psalm cxlix. 4. For the
Lord

Lord taketh pleasure in his people; he will beautify the meek with salvation. His Doctrine was something like this, viz: That the Salvation of Gods people mainly consists in Holiness. The name *Jesus* signifies *a Savior.* Jesus saves his people *from their Sins.* He renews them in the spirit of their minds — writes his Law in their hearts. Mr. Beacon ask'd a question. What is beauty — or, wherein does true beauty consist? He answer'd, in holiness — and said a great deal about it that I can't remember, & as aunt says she hant leisure now to help me any further — so I may just tell you a little that I remember without her assistance, and that I repeated to her yesterday at Tea — He said he would lastly address himself to the young people: My dear young friends, you are pleased with beauty, & like to be tho't beautifull — but let me tell ye, you 'l never be truly beautifull till you are like the King's daughter, all glorious within, all the orniments you can put on while your souls are unholy make you the more like white sepulchres garnish'd without, but full of deformyty within. You think me very unpolite

lite no doubt to address you in this manner, but I must go a little further and tell you, how cource soever it may sound to your delicacy, that while you are without holiness, your beauty is deformity — you are all over black & defil'd, ugly and loathsome to all holy beings, the wrath of ch' great God lie's upon you, & if you die in this condition, you will be turn'd into hell, with ugly devils, to eternity.

Nov. 27th. — We are very glad to see Mr. Gannett, because of him "we hear of your affairs & how you do "— as the apostle Paul once wrote. My unkle & aunt however, say they are sorry he is to be absent, so long as this whole winter, I *think*. I long now to have you come up — I want to see papa, mama, & brother, all most, for I cannot make any distinction which most — I should like to see Harry too. Mr. Gannett tells me he keeps a journal — I do want to see that — especially as Mr. Gannett has given me some specimens, as I may say of his "I and Aunt &c." I am glad Miss Jane is with you, I will write to her soon — Last monday I went with my aunt to visit Mrs. Beacon. I was exceedingly

exceedingly pleased with the visit, & so I *ought* to be, my aunt says, for there was much notice taken of me, particylarly by Mr. Beacon. I think I like him better every time I see him. I suppose he takes the kinder notice of me, because last thursday evening he was here, & when I was out of the room, aunt told him that I minded his preaching & could repeat what he said — I might have told you that notwithstanding the stir about the Proclamatien, we had an agreable Thanksgiven.   Mr. Hunt's [4] text was Psa. xcvii. i.   The LORD reigneth, — let the earth rejoice.   Mr. Beacon's text P M Psa. xxiv. i.   The earth is the LORD's & the fulness thereof.   My unkle & aunt Winslow [5] of Boston, their son & daughter, Master Daniel Mason (Aunt Winslows nephew from Newport, Rhode Island) & Miss Soley [6] spent the evening with us. We young folk had a room with a fire in it to ourselves.   Mr Beacon gave us his company for one hour. I spent Fryday with my friends in Sudbury Street.   I saw Mrs. Whitwell [7] very well yesterday, she was very glad of your Letter.

Nov. 28th. — I have your favor Hon^d
Mamma,

Mamma, by Mr. Gannett, & heartily thank you for the broad cloath, bags, ribbin & hat. The cloath & bags are both at work upon, & my aunt has bought a beautifull ermin trimming for my cloak. A C stands for Abigail Church. P F for Polly Frazior. I have presented one piece of ribbin to my aunt as you directed. She gives her love to you, & thanks you for it. I intend to send Nancy Mackky a pair of lace mittens, & the fag end of Harry's watch string. I hope Carolus (as papa us'd to call him) will think his daughter very smart with them. I am glad Hon^d madam, that you think my writing is better than it us'd to be — you see it is mended just here. I dont know what you mean by *terrible margins vaze.* I will endeavor to make my letters even for the future. Has Mary brought me any Lozong Mamma? I want to know whether I may give my old black quilt to Mrs Kuhn, for aunt sais, it is never worth while to take the pains to mend it again. Papa has wrote me a longer letter this time than you have Mad^m.

November the 29th. — My aunt Deming
gives

gives her love to you and says it is this morning 12 years since she had the pleasure of congratulating papa and you on the birth of your scribling daughter. She hopes if I live 12 years longer that I shall write and do everything better than can be expected in the *past* 12. I should be obliged to you, you will dismiss me for company.

30th Nov. — My company yesterday were

Miss Polly Deming,[8]
Miss Polly Glover,[9]
Miss Peggy Draper,
Miss Bessy Winslow,[10]
Miss Nancy Glover,[11]
Miss Sally Winslow [12]
Miss Polly Atwood,
Miss Han[h] Soley.

Miss Attwood as well as Miss Winslow are of this family. And Miss N. Glover did me honor by her presence, for she is older than cousin Sally and of her acquaintance. We made four couple at country dansing; danceing I mean. In the evening young Mr. Waters [13] hearing of my assembly, put his

his flute in his pocket and played several
minuets and other tunes, to which we danced
mighty cleverly. But Lucinda [14] was our
principal piper. Miss Church and Miss
Chaloner would have been here if sickness,
— and the Miss Sheafs,[15] if the death of
their father had not prevented. The black
Hatt I gratefully receive as your present,
but if Captain Jarvise had arrived here with
it about the time he sail'd from this place
for Cumberland it would have been of more
service to me, for I have been oblig'd to
borrow. I wore Miss Griswold's [16] Bonnet
on my journey to Portsmouth, & my cousin
Sallys Hatt ever since I came home, & now
I am to leave off my black ribbins tomorrow,
& am to put on my red cloak & black hatt
— I hope aunt wont let me wear the black
hatt with the red Dominie — for the people
will ask me what I have got to sell as I go
along street if I do, or, how the folk at New
guinie do? Dear mamma, you dont know
the fation here — I beg to look like other
folk. You dont know what a stir would be
made in sudbury street, were I to make my
appearance there in my red Dominie & black
Hatt.

Hatt.   But the old cloak & bonnett together
will make me a decent bonnett for common
ocation (I like that) aunt says, its a pitty
some of the ribbins you sent wont do for the
Bonnet.—I must now close up this Journal.
With Duty, Love, & Compliments as due,
perticularly to my Dear little brother (I long
to see him) & Mrs. Law, I will write to her
soon.

> I am Hon[d] Papa & mama,
>   Yr ever Dutiful Daughter
>   ANNE GREEN WINSLOW.

N. B.   My aunt Deming dont approve of
my English & has not the fear that you will
think her concernd in the Diction.

Dec[br]. 6th. — Yesterday I was prevented
dining at unkle Joshua's [17] by a snow storm
which lasted till 12 o'clock today, I spent
some part of yesterday afternoon and evening at Mr. Glovers.   When I came home,
the snow being so deep I was bro't home in
arms.   My aunt got Mr. Soley's Charlstown
to fetch me.   The snow is up to the peoples
wast in some places in the street.

Dec

Dec 14th. — The weather and walking have been very winter like since the above hotch-potch, pothooks & trammels. I went to Mrs. Whitwell's last wednessday — you taught me to spell the 4 day of the week, but my aunt says that it should be spelt wednesday. My aunt also says, that till I come out of an egregious fit of laughterre that is apt to sieze me & the violence of which I am at this present under, neither English sense, nor anything rational may be expected of me. I ment to say, that, I went to Mrs. Whitwell's to see Mad[m] Storers [18] funeral, the walking was very bad except on the sides of the street which was the reason I did not make a part of the procession. I should have dined with Mrs. Whitwell on thursday if a grand storm had not prevented, As she invited me. I saw Miss Caty Vans [19] at lecture last evening. I had a visit this morning from Mrs Dixon of Horton & Miss Polly Huston. Mrs Dixon is dissipointed at not finding her sister here.

Dec[r] 24th. — Elder Whitwell told my aunt, that this winter began as did the Winter of 1740. How that was I dont remember but this

this I know, that to-day is by far the coldest we have had since I have been in New England. (N. B. All run that are abroad.) Last sabbath being rainy I went to & from meeting in Mr. Soley's chaise. I dined at unkle Winslow's, the walking being so bad I rode there & back to meeting. Every drop that fell froze, so that from yesterday morning to this time the appearance has been similar to the discription I sent you last winter. The walking is so slippery & the air so cold, that aunt chuses to have me for her scoller these two days. And as tomorrow will be a holiday, so the pope and his associates have ordained,[20] my aunt thinks not to trouble Mrs Smith with me this week. I began a shift at home yesterday for myself, it is pretty forward. Last saturday was seven-night my aunt Suky[21] was delivered of a pretty little son, who was baptiz'd by Dr. Cooper[22] the next day by the name of Charles. I knew nothing of it till noonday, when I went there a visiting. Last Thursday I din'd & spent the afternoon at unkle Joshua's I should have gone to lecture with my aunt & heard our Mr Hunt preach, but

she

she would not wait till I came from writing
school. Miss Atwood, the last of our board-
ers, went off the same day. Miss Griswold
& Miss Meriam, having departed some time
agone, I forget whether I mention'd the
recept of Nancy's present. I am oblig'd to
her for it. The Dolphin is still whole. And
like to remain so.

Dec^r ⎰ This day, the extremity of the cold
27th ⎱ is somewhat abated. I keept Christmas at home this year, & did a very good
day's work, aunt says so. How notable I
have been this week I shall tell you by & by.
I spent the most part of Tuesday evening
with my favorite, Miss Soley, & as she is
confined by a cold & the weather still so
severe that I cannot git farther, I am to visit
her again before I sleep, & consult with her
(or rather she with me) upon a perticular
matter, which you shall know in its place.
How *strangely industrious* I have been this
week, I will inform you with my own hand
— at present, I am so dilligent, that I am
oblig'd to use the hand & pen of my old
friend, who being *near by* is better than a
brother *far off*. I dont forgit dear little
John

John Henry so pray mamma, dont mistake me.

Dec[r] ⟩ Last evening a little after 5 o'clock
28th ⟨ I finished my shift. I spent the evening at Mr. Soley's. I began my shift at 12 o'clock last monday, have read my bible every day this week & wrote every day save one.

Dec[r] ⟩ I return'd to my sewing school
30th ⟨ after a weeks absence, I have also paid my compliments to Master Holbrook.[23] Yesterday between meetings my aunt was call'd to Mrs. Water's [13] & about 8 in the evening Dr. Lloyd [24] brought little master to town (N. B. As a memorandum for myself. My aunt stuck a white sattan pincushin [25] for Mrs Waters.[13] On one side, is a plan-thorn with flowers, on the reverse, just un-der the border are, on one side stuck these words, Josiah Waters, then follows on the end, Dec[r] 1771, on the next side & end are the words, Welcome little Stranger.) Unkle has just come in & bro't one from me. I mean, unkle is just come in with a letter from Papa in his hand (& none for me) by way of Newbury. I am glad to hear that all

was

was well the 26 Nov[r] ult. I am told my
Papa has not mention'd me in this Letter.
Out of sight, out of mind. My aunt gives
her love to papa, & says that she will make
the necessary enquieries for my brother and
send you via. Halifax what directions and
wormseed she can collect.

1st Jan[y] ⟩ I wish my Papa, Mama, brother
  1772. ⟩ John Henry, & cousin Avery &
all the rest of my acquaintance at Cumberland, Fortlaurence, Barronsfield, Greenland,
Amherst &c. a Happy New Year, I have bestow'd no new year's gift,[26] as yet. But have
received one very handsome one, viz. the
History of Joseph Andrews abreviated. In
nice Guilt and flowers covers. This afternoon being a holiday I am going to pay my
compliments in Sudbury Street.

Jan[y] 4th ⟩ I was dress'd in my yellow coat,
  1772 ⟩ my black bib & apron, my pompedore[27] shoes, the cap my aunt Storer[28]
sometime since presented me with (blue
ribbins on it) & a very handsome loket in
the shape of a hart she gave me — the past
pin my Hon[d] Papa presented me with in my
cap, My new cloak & bonnet on, my pompedore

dore gloves, &c, &c. And I would tell you,
that *for the first time, they all lik'd my dress
very much.* My cloak & bonnett are really
very handsome, & so they had need be. For
they cost an amasing sight of money, not
quite £45 [29] tho' Aunt Suky said, that she
suppos'd Aunt Deming would be frighted
out of her Wits at the money it cost. I have
got *one* covering, by the cost, that is genteel,
& I like it much myself. On thursday I
attended my aunt to Lecture & heard Dr
Chauncey [30] preach a third sermon from Acts
ii. 42. They continued stedfastly — in break-
ing of bread. I din'd & spent the afternoon
at Mr. Whitwell's. Miss Caty Vans was one
of our company. Dr. Pemberton [31] & Dr
Cooper had on gowns, In the form of the
Episcopal cassock we hear, the Doct[s] design
to distinguish themselves from the inferior
clergy by these strange habits [at a time
too when the good people of N. E. are
threaten'd with & dreading the comeing of
an episcopal bishop] [32] N. B. I dont know
whether one sleeve would make a full trimm'd
negligee [33] as the fashion is at present, tho'
I cant say but it might make one of the fru-
gal

gal sort, with but scant triming. Unkle
says, they all have popes in their bellys.
Contrary to I. Peter v. 2. 3. Aunt says,
when she saw Dr P. roll up the pulpit stairs,
the figure of Parson Trulliber, recorded by
Mr Fielding occur'd to her mind & she was
really sorry a congregational divine, should,
by any instance whatever, give her so un-
pleasing an idea.

Jan^y ⎱ I have attended my schools every
11th ⎰ day this week except wednesday
afternoon. When I made a setting up visit
to aunt Suky, & was dress'd just as I was
to go to the ball. It cost me a pistoreen [34]
to nurse Eaton for tow cakes, which I took
care to eat before I paid for them. [35] I heard
Mr Thacher preach our Lecture last evening
Heb. 11. 3. I remember a great deal of the
sermon, but a'nt time to put it down. It is
one year last Sepr since he was ordain'd &
he will be 20 years of age next May if he
lives so long. I forgot that the weather
want fit for me to go to school last thursday.
I work'd at home.

Jan^y ⎱ I told you the 27th Ult that I was
17th ⎰ going to a constitation with miss
Soley.

Soley. I have now the pleasure to give you the result, viz. a very genteel well regulated assembly which we had at Mr Soley's last evening, miss Soley being mistress of the ceremony. Mrs Soley desired me to assist Miss Hannah in making out a list of guests which I did some time since, I wrote all the invitation cards. There was a large company assembled in a handsome, large, upper room in the new end of the house. We had two fiddles, & I had the honor to open the diversion of the evening in a minuet with miss Soley. — Here follows a list of the company as we form'd for country dancing.

Miss Soley &	Miss Anna Greene Winslow
Miss Calif	Miss Scott
Miss Williams	Miss McCarthy
Miss Codman	Miss Winslow
Miss Ives	Miss Coffin
Miss Scolley [36]	Miss Bella Coffin [37]
Miss Waldow	Miss Quinsy [38]
Miss Glover	Miss Draper
Miss Hubbard	

Miss Cregur (usually pronounced Kicker) & two Miss Sheafs were invited but were sick

sick or sorry & beg'd to be excus'd. There was a little Miss Russell & the little ones of the family present who could not dance. As spectators, there were Mr & Mrs Deming, Mr. & Mrs Sweetser Mr & Mrs Soley, Mr & Miss Cary, Mrs Draper, Miss Oriac, Miss Hannah — our treat was nuts, rasins, Cakes, Wine, punch,[39] hot & cold, all in great plenty. We had a very agreeable evening from 5 to 10 o'clock. For variety we woo'd a widow, hunted the whistle, threaded the needle, & while the company was collecting, we diverted ourselves with playing of pawns, no rudeness Mamma I assure you. Aunt Deming desires you would *perticulary observe*, that the elderly part of the company were *spectators only*, they mix'd not in either of the above describ'd scenes.

I was dress'd in my yellow coat, black bib & apron, black feathers on my head, my past comb, & all my past [40] garnet marquesett [41] & jet pins, together with my silver plume — my loket, rings, black collar round my neck, black mitts & 2 or 3 yards of blue ribbin, (black & blue is high tast) striped tucker and ruffels (not my best) & my silk shoes compleated my dress. Jan[y]

Jan^y ⎰   Yesterday I had an invitation to
18th ⎱ celebrate Miss Caty's birth-day with
her.   She gave it me the night before.   Miss
is 10 years old.   The best dancer in Mr
Turners [42] school, she has been his scoller
these 3 years.   My aunt thought it proper
(as our family had a invitation) that I should
attend a neighbor's funeral yesterday P. M.
I went directly from it to Miss Caty's Rout
& arriv'd ex   .   .   .   .   .   .

BOSTON January 25 1772.

Hon'^d Mamma, My Hon'^d Papa has never
signified to me his approbation of my journals, from whence I infer, that he either
never reads them, or does not give himself
the trouble to remember any of their contents, tho' some part has been address'd to
him, so, for the future, I shall trouble only
you with this part of my scribble — Last
thursday I din'd at Unkle Storer's & spent
the afternoon in that neighborhood.   I met
with some adventures in my way viz.   As I
was going, I was overtaken by a lady who
was quite a stranger to me.   She accosted me
with "how do you do miss?"   I answer'd
her,

her, but told her I had not the pleasure of knowing her. She then ask'd " what is your name miss? I believe you think 't is a very strange questian to ask, but have a mind to know." Nanny Green — She interrupted me with " not Mrs. Winslow of Cumberland's daughter." Yes madam I am. When did you hear from your Mamma? how do's she do? When shall you write to her? When you do, tell her that you was overtaken in the street by her old friend Mrs Login, give my love to her & tell her she must come up soon & live on Jamaca plain. we have got a nice meeting-house, & a charming minister, & all so cleaver. She told me she had ask'd Unkle Harry to bring me to see her, & he said he would. Her minister is Mr Gordon. I have heard him preach several times at the O. South. In the course of my peregrination, as aunt calls it, I happen'd in to a house where D—— was attending the Lady of the family. How long she was at his opperation, I know not. I saw him twist & tug & pick & cut off whole locks of grey hair at a slice (the lady telling him she would have no hair to dress next time) for the

the space of a hour & a half, when I left them, he seeming not to be near done. This lady is not a grandmother tho' she is both old enough & grey enough to be one.

Jan^y ⎰ I spent yesterday with Aunt Storer,
31 ⎱ except a little while I was at Aunt Sukey's with Mrs Barrett dress'd in a white brocade, & cousin Betsey dress'd in a red lutestring, both adorn'd with past, perls marquesett &c. They were after tea escorted by Mr. Newton & Mr Barrett to ye assembly at Concert Hall. This is a snowy day, & I am prevented going to school.

Feb. 9th. — My honored Mamma will be so good as to excuse my useing the pen of my old friend just here, because I am disabled by a whitloe on my fourth finger & something like one on my middle finger, from using my own pen; but altho' my right hand is in bondage, my left is free; & my aunt says, it will be a nice oppertunity if I do but improve it, to perfect myself in learning to spin flax. I am pleased with the proposal & am at this present, exerting myself for this purpose. I hope, when two, or at most three months are past, to give you occular demon-

stration

WEDDING PARTY IN BOSTON IN 1756

stration of my proficiency in *this art,* as well as several others. My fingers are not the only part of me that has suffer'd with sores within this fortnight, for I have had an ugly great boil upon my right hip & about a dozen small ones — I am at present swath'd hip & thigh, as Samson smote the Philistines, but my soreness is near over. My aunt thought it highly proper to give me some cooling physick, so last tuesday I took 1-2 oz Globe Salt (a disagreeable potion) & kept chamber. Since which, there has been no new erruption, & a great alteration for the better in those I had before.

I have read my bible to my aunt this morning (as is the daily custom) & sometimes I read other books to her. So you may perceive, I *have the use of my tongue* & I tell her it is a good thing to have the use of my tongue. Unkle Ned [43] called here just now — all well — by the way he is come to live in Boston again, & till he can be better accomodated, is at housekeeping where Mad^m Storer lately lived, he is looking for a less house. I tell my Aunt I feel a disposician to be a good girl, & she pleases herself
that

that she shall have much comfort of me to-day, which as cousin Sally is ironing we expect to have to ourselves.

Feb. 10th. — This day I paid my respects to Master Holbrook, after a week's absence, my finger is still in limbo as you may see by the writeing. I have not paid my compliments to Madam Smith,[44] for, altho' I can drive the goos quill a bit, I cannot so well manage the needle. So I will lay my hand to the distaff, as the virtuous woman did of old — Yesterday was very bad weather, neither aunt, nor niece at publick worship.

Feb. 12th. — Yesterday afternoon I spent at unkle Joshuas. Aunt Green gave me a plaister for my fingure that has near cur'd it, but I have a new boil, which is under poultice, & tomorrow I am to undergo another seasoning with globe Salt. The following lines Aunt Deming found in grandmama Sargent's[45] pocket-book & gives me leave to copy 'em here. —

> Dim eyes, deaf ears, cold stomach shew,
> My dissolution is in view
> The shuttle's thrown, my race is run,
> My sun is set, my work is done;
> My span is out, my tale is told,

My

> My flower's decay'd, & stock grows old,
> The dream is past, the shadows fled,
> My soul now longs for Christ my head,
> I've lived to seventy six or nigh,
> GOD calls at last, & now I'll die.[46]

My honor'd Grandma departed this vale of tears 1-4 before 4 o'clock wednesday morning August 21, 1771. Aged 74 years, 2 months & ten days.

Feb. 13th. — Everybody says that this is a bitter cold day, but I know nothing about it but hearsay for I am in aunt's chamber (which is very warm always) with a nice fire, a stove, sitting in Aunt's easy chair, with a tall three leav'd screen at my back, & I am very comfortable. I took my second (& I hope last) potion of Globe salts this morning. I went to see Aunt Storer yesterday afternoon, & by the way Unkle Storer is so ill that he keeps chamber. As I went down I call'd at Mrs Whitwell's & must tell you Mr & Mrs Whitwell are both ill. Mrs. Whitwell with the rheumatism. I saw Madm Harris, Mrs Mason and Miss Polly Vans [47] there, they all give their love to you — Last evening I went to catechizing with Aunt. Our ministers have

have agreed during the long evenings to discourse upon the questions or some of 'em in
the assembly's shorter catechism, taking 'em
in their order at the house of Mrs Rogers
in School Street, every wednesday evening.
Mr. Hunt began with the first question and
shew'd what it is to glorify GOD. Mr
Bacon then took the second, what rule &c.
which he has spent three evenings upon, &
now finished. Mr Hunt having taken his
turn to show what the Scriptures principly
teach, & what is GOD. I remember he said
that there was nothing properly done without a rule, & he said that the rule God had
given us to glorify him by was the bible.
How miraculously (said he) has God pre-
serv'd this blessed book. It was once in the
reign of a heathen emperor condemn'd to be
burnt, at which time it was death to have a
bible & conceal it, but God's providence was
wonderful in preserving it when so much
human policy had been exerted to bury it in
Oblivion — but for all that, here we have it
as pure & uncorrupted as ever — many books
of human composure have had much pains
taken to preserve 'em, notwithstanding they
are

are buried in Oblivion. He considered who was the author of the bible, he prov'd that GOD was the author, for no *good* man could be the author, because such a one would not be guilty of imposition, & an evil man could not unless we suppose a house divided against itself. he said a great deal more to prove the bible is certainly the word of God from the matter it contains &c, but the best evidence of the truth of divine revelation, every true believer has in his own heart. This he said, the natural man had no idea of. I did not understand all he said about the external and internal evidence, but this I can say, that I understand him better than any body else that I hear preach. Aunt has been down stairs all the time I have been recolecting & writeing this. Therefore, all this of own head, of consequence.

Valentine day.[48] — My cousin Sally reeled off a 10 knot skane of yarn today. My valentine was an old country plow-joger. The yarn was of my spinning. Aunt says it will do for filling. Aunt also says niece is a whimsical child.

Feb. 17. — Since wednesday evening, I have

have not been abroad since yesterday afternoon. I went to meeting & back in Mr. Soley's chaise. Mr. Hunt preached. He said that human nature is as opposite to God as darkness to light. That our sin is only bounded by the narrowness of our capacity. His text was Isa. xli. 14. 18. The mountains &c. He said were unbelief, pride, covetousness, enmity, &c. &c. &c. This morning I took a walk for Aunt as far as Mr. Soley's. I called at Mrs Whitwell's & found the good man & lady both better than when I saw them last. On my return I found Mr. Hunt on a visit to aunt. After the usual salutations & when did you hear from your papa &c. I ask'd him if the blessing pronounced by the minister before the congregation is dismissed, is not a part of the publick worship? "Yes."

"Why then, do you Sir, say, let us conclude the publick worship by singing?" "Because singing is the last act in which the whole congregation is unanimously to join. The minister in Gods name blesses his i. e. Gods people agreeable to the practice of the apostles, who generally close the
epistles

epistles with a benediction in the name of
the Trinity, to which, Amen is subjoined,
which, tho' pronounc'd by the minister, is,
or ought to be the sentiment & prayer of
the whole assembly, the meaning whereof
is, So be it."

Feb. 18th. — Another ten knot skane of
my yarn was reel'd off today. Aunt says
it is very good. My boils & whitloes are
growing well apace, so that I can knit a
little in the evening.

Transcribed from the Boston Evening
Post :

Sep. 18, 1771. Under the head of London news, you may find that last Thursday
was married at Worcester the Widow Biddle
of Wellsburn in the county of Warwick, to
her grandson John Biddle of the same place,
aged twenty three years. It is very remarkable. the widdow had one son & one daughter ; 18 grandchildren & 5 great grandchildren ; her present husband has one daughter,
who was her great granddaughter but is now
become her daughter ; her other great grandchildren are become her cousins ; her grandchildren her brothers & sisters ; her son &
daughter

daughter her father & mother. I think! tis the most extraordinary account I ever read in a News-Paper. It will serve to puzzel Harry Dering with.

Monday Feb. 18th. — Bitter cold. I am just come from writing school. Last Wednesday P. M. while I was at school Aunt Storer called in to see Aunt Deming in her way to Mr Inches's. She walk'd all that long way. Thursday last I din'd & spent the afternoon with Aunt Sukey. I attended both my schools in the morning of that day. I cal'd at unkle Joshua's as I went along, as I generally do, when I go in town, it being all in my way. Saterday I din'd at Unkle Storer's, drank tea at Cousin Barrel's, was entertain'd in the afternoon with scating. Unkle Henry was there. Yesterday by the help of neighbor Soley's Chaise, I was at meeting all day, tho' it snow'd in the afternoon. I might have say'd I was at Unkle Winslow's last Thursday Eveg & when I inform you that my needle work at school, & knitting at home, went on *as usual,* I think I have laid before you a pretty full account of the last week. You see how I improve in my writing, but I drive on as fast as I can.   Feb.

Feb. 21 ⟨ This day Jack Frost bites
Thursday. ⟩ very hard, so hard aunt won't
let me go to any school. I have this morning made part of a coppy with the very pen
I have now in my hand, writting this with.
Yesterday was so cold there was a very
thick vapor upon the water, but I attended
my schools all day. My unkle says yesterday was 10 degrees colder than any day we
have had before this winter. And my aunt
says she believes this day is 10 degrees
colder than it was yesterday ; & moreover,
that she would not put a dog out of doors.
The sun gives forth his rays through a
vapor like that which was upon the water
yesterday. But Aunt bids me give her love
to pappa & all the family & tell them that
she should be glad of their company in her
warm parlour, indeed there is not one room
in this house but is very warm when there
is a good fire in them. As there is in this
at present. Yesterday I got leave (by my
aunt's desire) to go from school at 4 o'clock
to see my unkle Ned who has had the mis-
fortune to break his leg. I call'd in to warm
myself at unkle Joshua's. Aunt Hannah told
me

me I had better not go any further for she
could tell me all about him, so I say'd as it
is so cold I believe aunt won't be angry so
I will stay, I therefore took off my things,
aunt gave me leave to call at Unkle Joshua's
& was very glad I went no further. Aunt
Hannah told me he was as well as could be
expected for one that has a broken bone.
He was coming from Watertown in a chaise
the horse fell down on the Hill, this side
Mr Brindley's. he was afraid if he fell out,
the wheel would run over him, he therefore
gave a start & fell out & broke his leg, the
horse strugled to get up, but could not.
unkle Ned was affraid if he did get up the
chaise wheels would run over him, so he
went on his two hands and his other foot
drawing his lame leg after him & got behind
the chaise, (so he was safe) & there lay in
the snow for some time, nobody being near.
at last 2 genteelmen came, they tho't the
horse was dead when they first saw him
at a distance, but hearing somebody hollow,
went up to it. By this time there was a
countraman come along, the person that hollow'd was unkle Ned. They got a slay and
put

put him in it with some hay and a blanket,
wrapt him up well as they could & brought
him to Deacon Smith's in town. Now Papa
& Mamma, this hill is in Brookline. And
now again, I have been better inform'd for
the hill is in Roxbury & poor Unkle Ned
was alone in the chaise. Both bones of his
leg are broke, but they did not come thro' the
skin, which is a happy circumstance. It is
his right leg that is broke. My Grandmamma
sent Miss Deming, Miss Winslow & I one
eighth of a Dollar a piece for a New Years
gift. My Aunt Deming & Miss Deming had
letters from Grandmamma. She was pretty
well, she wrote aunt that Mrs Marting was
brought to bed with a son Joshua about a
month since, & is with her son very well.
Grandmamma was very well last week. I
have made the purchase I told you of a few
pages agone, that is, last Thursday I purchas'd with my aunt Deming's leave, a very
beautiful white feather hat, that is, the out
side, which is a bit of white hollond with the
feathers sew'd on in a most curious manner
white & unsullyed as the falling snow, this
hat I have long been saving my money to
procure

procure for which I have let your kind allow-
ance, Papa, lay in my aunt's hands till this
hat which I spoke for was brought home.
As I am (as we say) a daughter of liberty [49]
I chuse to wear as much of our own manu-
factory as pocible. But my aunt says, I
have wrote this account very badly. I will
go on to save my money for a chip & a
lineing &c.

Papa I rec'd your letter dated Jan. 11, for
which I thank you, Sir, & thank you greatly
for the money I received therewith. I am
very glad to hear that Brother John papa &
mamma & cousin are well. I 'll answer your
letter papa and yours mamma and cousin
Harry's too. I am very glad mamma your
eyes are better. I hope by the time I have
the pleasure of hearing from Cumberland
again your eyes will be so well that you will
favor me with one from you.

Feb. 22ᵈ. — Since about the middle of December, ult. we have had till this week, a
series of cold and stormy weather — every
snow storm (of which we have had abun-
dance) except the first, ended with rain, by
which means the snow was so hardened that
strong

strong gales at N W soon turned it, & all
above ground to ice, which this day seven-
night was from one to three, four & they
say, in some places, five feet thick, in the
streets of this town. Last saturday morning we had a snow storm come on, which
continued till four o'clock P. M. when it
turned to rain, since which we have had a
warm air, with many showers of rain, one
this morning a little before day attended
with thunder. The streets have been very
wet, the water running like rivers all this
week, so that I could not possibly go to
school, neither have I yet got the bandage
off my fingure. Since I have been writing
now, the wind suddenly sprung up at N W
and blew with violence so that we may get to
meeting to-morrow, perhaps on dry ground.
Unkle Ned was here just now & has fairly
or unfairly carried off aunt's cut paper pictures,[50] tho' she told him she had given
them to papa some years ago. It has been
a very sickly time here, not one person that
I know of but has been under heavy colds
— (all laid up at unkle Storer's) in general
got abroad again. Aunt Suky had not been
down

down stairs since her lying in, when I last saw her, but I hear she is got down. She has had a broken breast. I have spun 30 knots of linning yarn, and (partly) new footed a pair of stockings for Lucinda, read a part of the pilgrim's progress, coppied part of my text journal (that if I live a few years longer, I may be able to understand it, for aunt sais, that to her, the contents as I first mark'd them, were an impenetrable secret) play'd some, tuck'd a great deal (Aunt Deming says it is very true) laugh'd enough, & I tell aunt it is all human *nature*, if not human reason. And now, I wish my honored mamma a very good night.

Saturday noon Feb. 23ᵈ } Dear Pappa, do's the winter continue as pleasant at Cumberland as when you wrote to me last? We had but very little winter here, till February came in, but we have little else since. The cold still continues tho' not so extreme as it was last Thursday. I have attended my schools all this week except one day, and am going as soon as I have din'd to see how Unkle Ned does. I was thinking, Sir, to lay up a piece of money you sent me, but

as

GENERAL JOSHUA WINSLOW

as you sent it to me to lay out I have a mind
to buy a chip & linning for my feather hatt.
But my aunt says she will think of it. My
aunt says if I behave myself very well indeed, not else, she will give me a garland of
flowers to orniment it, tho' she has layd
aside the biziness of flower making.[51]

Feb. 25th. — This is a very stormy day of
snow, hail & rain, so that I cannot get to
Master Holbrook's, therefore I will here copy
something I lately transcribed on a loose
paper from Dr. Owen's sermon on Hab. iii,
1, 2, 3, 4, 5, 6, 7, 8, 9. "I have heard that
a full wind behind the ship drives her not
so fast forward, as a side wind, that seems
almost as much against her as with her; &
the reason they say is, because a full wind
fills but some of her sails.

Wednesday. — Very cold, but this morning
I was at sewing and writing school, this afternoon all sewing, for Master Holbrook does
not in the winter keep school of afternoons.
Unkle Henrys feet are so much better that
he wears shoos now.

Monday

Monday ⎫ I have been to writing school
noon ⎬ this morning and Sewing. The
Feb. 25th. ⎭ day being very pleasant, very
little wind stirring. Jemima called to see
me last evening. She lives at Master Jimmy
Lovel's.[52] Dear mamma, I suppose that you
would be glad to hear that Betty Smith who
has given you so much trouble, is well &
behaves herself well & I should be glad if
I could write you so. But the truth is, no
sooner was the 29th Regiment encamp'd
upon the common but miss Betty took herself among them (as the Irish say) & there
she stay'd with Bill Pinchion & awhile. The
next news of her was, that she was got into
gaol for stealing: from whence she was
taken to the publick whipping post.[53] The
next adventure was to the Castle, after the
soldier's were remov'd there, for the murder
of the 5th March last.[54] When they turn'd
her away from there, she came up to town
again, and soon got into the workhouse for
new misdemeanours, she soon ran away from
there and sit up her old trade of pilfering
again, for which she was put a second time
into gaol, there she still remains. About
two

two months agone (as well as I can remember) she & a number of her wretched companions set the gaol on fire, in order to get out, but the fire was timely discovered & extinguished, & there, as I said she still remains till this day, in order to be tried for her crimes. I heard somebody say that as she has some connections with the army no doubt but she would be cleared, and perhaps, have a pension into the bargain. Mr. Henry says the way of sin is down hill, when persons get into that way they are not easily stopped.

Feb. 27. — This day being too stormy for me to go to any school, and nothing as yet having happen'd that is worth your notice, my aunt gives me leave to communicate to you something that much pleas'd her when she heard of it, & which I hope will please you my Papa and Mamma. I believe I may have inform'd you that since I have been in Boston, Dr. Byles [55] has pretty frequently preached & sometimes administer'd the sacrament, when our Candidates have preached to the O. S. Church, because they are not tho't qualified to administer Gospel Ordinance,

nance, till they be settled Pastours.   About two months ago a brother of the church sent Dr Byles a Card which contain'd after the usual introduction, the following words, Mr W—— dont set up for an Expositor of Scripture, yet ventures to send Dr. Byles a short comment on 1 Cor. ix. 11. which he thinks agreeable to the genuine import of the text, & hopes the Dr will not disapprove it. The comment was a dozen pounds of Chocolate &c. — To which the D[r] return'd the following very pretty answer.   D[r] Byles returns respects to Mr W & most heartily thanks him for his judicious practical Familie Expositer, which is in Tast.   My aunt Deming gives her love to you mamma, and bids me tell you, as a matter you will be very glad to know, that D[r] Byles & his lady & family, have enjoy'd a good share of health & perfect harmony for several years past.

Mr Beacon is come home.   My unkle Neddy is very comfortable, has very little pain, & know fever with his broken bone. My Unkle Harry [56] was here yesterday & is very well.   Poor Mrs Inches is dangerously ill of a fever.   We have not heard how she does today.   March

March 4th. — Poor Mrs Inches is dead. Gone from a world of trouble, as she has left this to her poor mother. Aunt says she heartyly pities Mrs Jackson. Mr Nat. Bethune died this morning, Mrs Inches last night.

We had the greatest fall of snow yesterday we have had this winter. Yet cousin Sally, miss Polly, & I rode to & from meeting in Mr Soley's chaise both forenoon & afternoon, & with a stove [57] was very comfortable there. If brother John is as well and hearty as cousin Frank, he is a clever boy. Unkle Neddy continues very comfortable. I saw him last saturday. I have just now been writing four lines in my Book almost as well as the copy. But all the intreaties in the world will not prevail upon me to do always as well as I can, which is not the least trouble to me, tho' its a great grief to aunt Deming. And she says by writing so frightfully above.

March 6. — I think the appearance this morning is as winterish as any I can remember, earth, houses, trees, all covered with snow, which began to fall yesterday morning

&

& continued falling all last night. The Sun now shines very bright, the N. W. wind blows very fresh. Mr Gannett din'd here yesterday, from him, my unkle, aunt & cousin Sally, I had an account of yesterday's pub-lick performances,[58] & exhibitions, but aunt says I need not write about 'em because, no doubt there will be printed accounts. I should have been glad if I could have seen & heard for myselfe. My face is better, but I have got a heavy cold yet.

March 9th. — After being confined a week, I rode yesterday afternoon to & from meet-ing in Mr Soley's chaise. I got no cold and am pretty well today. This has been a very snowy day today. Any body that sees this may see that I have wrote nonsense but Aunt says, I have been a very good girl to day about my work however — I think this day's work may be called a piece meal for in the first place I sew'd on the bosom of unkle's shirt, mended two pair of gloves, mended for the wash two handkerchiefs, (one cambrick) sewed on half a border of a lawn apron of aunts, read part of the xxist chapter of Exodous, & a story in the Mother's gift.

Now,

Now, Hon^d Mamma, I must tell you of something that happened to me to-day, that has not happen'd before this great while, viz My Unkle & Aunt both told me, I was a very good girl. Mr Gannett gave us the favour of his company a little while this morning (our head). I have been writing all the above gibberish while aunt has been looking after her family — now she is out of the room — now she is in — & takes up my pen in *my* absence to observe, I am a little simpleton for informing my mamma, that it is *a great while* since I was prais'd because she will conclude that it is *a great while* since I deserv'd to be prais'd. I will henceforth try to observe their praise & yours too. I mean deserve. It 's now tea time — as soon as that is over, I shall spend the rest of the evening in reading to my aunt. It is near candle lighting.

March 10, 5 o'clock P. M. — I have finish'd my stent of sewing work for this day & wrote a billet to Miss Caty Vans, a copy of which I shall write on the next page. To-morrow if the weather is fit I am to visit. I have again been told I was a good girl.
My

My Billet to Miss Vans was in the following words. Miss Green gives her compliments to Miss Vans, and informs her that her aunt Deming quite misunderstood the matter about the queen's night-Cap.[59] Mrs. Deming thou't that it was a black skull cap linn'd with red that Miss Vans ment which she thou't would not be becoming to Miss Green's light complexion. Miss Green now takes the liberty to send the materials for the Cap Miss Vans was so kind as to say she would make for her, which, when done, she engages to take special care of for Miss Vans' sake. Mrs. Deming joins her compliments with Miss Green's — they both wish for the pleasure of a visit from Miss Vans. Miss Soley is just come in to visit me & 'tis near dark.

March 11. — Boast not thyself of tomorrow ; for thou knowest not what a day may bring forth. Thus king Solomon, inspired by the Holy Ghost, cautions, Pro. xxvii. 1. My aunt says, this is a most necessary lesson to be learn'd & laid up in the heart. I am quite of her mind. I have met with a disappointment to day, & aunt says, I may look for

for them every day — we live in a changing
world — in scripture call'd a vale of tears.
Uncle said yesterday that there had not been
so much snow on the ground this winter as
there was then — it has been vastly added
to since then, & is now 7 feet deep in some
places round this house ; it is above the fence
in the coart & thick snow began to fall and
condtinu'd till about 5 o'clock P. M. (it is
about 1-4 past 8 o'clock) since which there
has been a steady rain — so no visiting as I
hoped this day, & this is the disappointment
I mentioned on t'other page.   Last saturday
I sent my cousin Betsy Storer a Billet of
which the following is a copy.   Miss Green
gives her love to Miss Storer & informs
her that she is very *sensible* of the effects
of a bad cold, not only in the pain she has
had in her throat, neck and face, which have
been much swell'd & which she is not quite
clear of, but that she has also been by the
same depriv'd of the pleasure of seeing
Miss Storer & her other friends in Sudbury
Street.   She begs, her Duty, Love & Compliments, may be presented as due & that
she may be inform'd if they be in health.

To

To this I have receiv'd no answer. I suppose she don't think I am worth an answer. But I have finished my stent, and wrote all under this date, & now I have just daylight eno' to add, my love and duty to dear friends at *Cumberland*.

March 14. — Mr. Stephen March, at whose house I was treated so kindly last fall, departed this life last week, after languishing several months under a complication of disorders — we have not had perticulars, therefore cannot inform you, whether he engag'd the King of terrors with christian fortitude, or otherwise.

> " Stoop down my Thoughts, that use to rise,
>   Converse a while with Death ;
>   Think how a gasping Mortal lies,
>   And pants away his Breath."

Last Thursday I din'd with unkle Storer, & family at aunt Sukey's — all well except Charles Storer who was not so ill but what, *that* I mean, he din'd with us. Aunt Suky's Charles is a pretty little boy & grows nicely. We were diverted in the afternoon with an account of a queer Feast that had been made that day in a certain Court of this town for the

EBENEZER STORER

the Entertainment of a number of Tories —
perhaps seventeen. One contain'd three
calves heads (skin off) with their appurti-
nencies anciently call'd pluck — Their other
dish (for they had but two) contain'd a number of roast fowls — half a dozen, we suppose,* & all roosters at this season no doubt.
Yesterday, soon after I came from writing
school we had another snow storm begun,
which continued till after I went to bed.
This morning the sun shines clear (so it did
yesterday morning till 10 o'clock.) It is now
bitter cold, & such a quantity of snow upon
the ground, as the Old people don't remember
ever to have seen before at this time of the
year. My aunt Deming says, when she first
look'd abroad this morning she felt anxious
for her brother, & his family at Cumberland,
fearing lest they were covered up in snow.
It is now 1-2 after 12 o'clock noon. The
sun has been shineing in his full strength
for full 6 hours, & the snow not melted
enough anywhere in sight of this house, to
cause one drop of water.

March 17. — Yesterday, I went to see
aunt

* There was six as I have since heard.

aunt Polly, & finding her going out, I spent the afternoon with aunt Hannah. While I was out, a snow storm overtook me. This being a fine sun shine (tho' cold) day I have been to writing school, & wrote two pieces, one I presented to aunt Deming, and the other I design for my Honor'd Papa, I hope he will approve of it. I sent a piece of my writing to you Hon'd Mamma last fall, which I hope you receiv'd. When my aunt Deming was a little girl my Grandmamma Sargent told her the following story viz. One Mr. Calf who had three times enjoy'd the Mayorality of the city of London, had after his decease, a monoment erected to his memory with the following inscription on it.

> Here lies buried the body of
>   Sir Richard Calf,
> Thrice Lord Mayor of London.
>   Honor, Honor, Honor.

A drol gentleman passing by with a bit of chalk in his hand underwrote thus —

> O cruel death ! more subtle than a Fox
> That would not let this Calf become an Ox,
> That he might browze among the briers & thorns
> And with his brethren wear,
> Horns. Horns. Horns.

My

My aunt told me the foregoing some time since & today I ask'd her leave to insert it in my journal. My aunt gives her love to you & directs me to tell you that she tho't my piece of linnin would have made me a dozen of shifts but she could cut no more than ten out of it. There is some left, but not enough for another. Nine of them are finish'd wash'd & iron'd ; & the other would have been long since done if my fingers had not been sore. My cousin Sally made three of them for me, but then I made two shirts & part of another for unkle to help her. I believe unless something remarkable should happen, such as a *warm day*, my mamma will consent that I dedicate a few of my next essays to papa. I think the second thing I said to aunt this morning was, that I intended to be *very good all day.* To make this out,

" Next unto *God*, dear Parents I address
  Myself to you in humble Thankfulness,
" For all your Care & Charge on me bestow'd ;
" The means of Learning unto me allow'd,
" Go on I pray, & let me still pursue
" Those Golden ARTS the Vulgar never knew."

Yr Dutifull Daughter
ANNA GREEN WINSLOW.
The

The poetry I transcrib'd from my Copy Book.

March 19.—Thursday last I spent at home, except a quarter of an hour between sunset and dark, I stepped over the way to Mr. Glover's with aunt.   Yesterday I spent at Unkle Neddy's & stitched wristbands for aunt Polly. By the way, I must inform you, (pray dont let papa see this) that yesterday I put on No 1 of my new shifts, & indeed it is very comfortable.   It is *long* since I had a shift to my *back*.   I dont know if I ever ha'd till now — It seem'd so strange too, to have any linen below my waist — I am going to dine at Mrs. Whitwell's to day, by invitation.   I spent last evening at Mrs Rogers. Mr Hunt discoursed upon the doctrine of the Trinity — it was the second time that he spoke upon the subject at that place.   I did not hear him the first time.   His business last eve[g] was to prove the divinity of the Son, & holy Ghost, & their equality with the Father.   My aunt Deming says, it is a grief to her, that I don't always write as well as I can, *I can write pretily*.

March 21. — I din'd & spent the afternoon
of

of Thursday last, at Mrs Whitwell's. Mrs
Lathrop, & Mrs Carpenter din'd there also.
The latter said she was formerly acquainted
with mamma, ask'd how she did, & when I
heard from her, — said, I look'd much like
her. Madam Harris & Miss P. Vans were
also of the company. While I was abroad
the snow melted to such a degree, that my
aunt was oblig'd to get Mr Soley's chaise to
bring me home. Yesterday, we had by far
the gratest storm of wind & snow that there
has been this winter. It began to fall yesterday morning & continued falling till after
our family were in bed. (P. M.) Mr. Hunt
call'd in to visit us just after we rose from
diner ; he ask'd me, whether I had heard
from my papa & mamma, since I wrote 'em.
He was answer'd, no sir, it would be strange
if ᴛ had because I had been writing to 'em
today, & indeed so I did every day. Aunt
told him that *his name* went frequently into
my journals together with broken & some
times whole sentences of his sermons, conversations &c. He laugh'd & call'd me News-
monger, & said I was a daily advertiser. He
added, that he did not doubt but my journals
afforded

afforded much entertainment & would be a future benefit &c. Here is a fine compliment for me mamma.

March 26. — Yesterday at 6 o'clock, I went to Unkle Winslow's, their neighbor Greenleaf was their. She said she knew Mamma, & that I look like her. Speaking about papa & you occation'd Unkle Winslow to tell me that he had kiss'd you long before papa knew you. From thence we went to Miss Rogers's where, to a full assembly Mr Bacon read his 3ᵈ sermon on R. iv. 6, I can remember he said, that, before we all sinned in Adam our father, Christ loved us. He said the Son of God always did as his father gave him commandment, & to prove this, he said, that above 17 hundred years ago he left the bosom of the Father, & came & took up his abode with men, & bore all the scourgings & buffetings which the vile Jews inflicted on him, & then was hung upon the accursed tree — he died, was buried, & in three days rose again — ascended up to heaven & there took his seat at the right hand of the Majesty on high from whence he will come to be the supream and impartial

judge

judge of quick & dead — and when his poor
Mother & her poor husband went to Jerusa-
lem to keep the passover & he went with
them, he disputed among the doctors, &
when his Mother ask'd him about it he
said "wist ye not that I must be about my
Father's business," — all this he said was a
part of that wrighteousness for the sake of
which a sinner is justafied — Aunt has been
up stairs all the time I have been writeing &
recollecting this — so no help from her. She
is come down now & I have been reading
this over to her. She sais, she is glad I remember so much, but I have not done the
subject justice. She sais I have blended
things somewhat improperly — an interup-
tion by company.

March 28. — Unkle Harry was here last
evening & inform'd us that by a vessel from
Halifax which arriv'd yesterday, Mr H Newton, inform'd his brother Mr J Newton of
the sudden death of their brother Hibbert
in your family 21 January ult. (Just five
months to a day since Grandmamma Sargent's death.) With all the circumstances
relating to it. My aunt Deming gives her
love

love to Mamma & wishes her a sanctified
improvement of all God's dealings with her,
& that it would please him to bring her & all
the family safe to Boston.   Jarvis is put up
for Cumberland, we hope he will be there by
or before Mayday.   This minute I have receiv'd my queen's night cap from Miss Caty
Vans — we like it.   Aunt says, that if the
materials it is made of were more substantial
than gauze, it might serve occationally to
hold any thing mesur'd by an 1-2 peck, but it
is just as it should be, & very decent, & she
wishes my writing was *as* decent.   But I got
into one of my frolicks, upon sight of the Cap.

April 1st. — Will you be offended mamma,
if I ask you, if you remember the flock of wild
Geese that papa call'd you to see flying over
the Blacksmith's shop this day three years ?
I hope not ; I only mean to divert you.   The
snow is near gone in the street before us,
& mud supplies the place thereof ; After a
week's absence, I this day attended Master
Holbrook with some difficulty, what was last
week a pond is to-day a quag, thro' which I
got safe however, & if aunt * had known it
was

* Miss Green tells her aunt, that the word refer'd to be-
gins with a dipthong.

was so bad, she sais she would not have sent me, but I neither wet my feet, nor drabled my clothes, indeed I have but one garment that I could contrive to drabble.

N. B. It is 1 April.

April 3. — Yesterday was the annual Fast, & I was at meeting all day. Mr Hunt preach'd A. M. from Zac. vii. 4, 5, 6, 7. He said, that if we did not mean as we said in pray's it was only a compliment put upon God, which was a high affront to his divine Majesty. Mr Bacon, P. M. from James v. 17. He said, "pray's, effectual & fervent, might be, where there were no words, but there might be elegant words where there is no prayr's. The essence of pray's consists in offering up holy desires to God agreeable to his will, — it is the flowing out of gracious affections — what then are the pray'rs of an unrenewed heart that is full of enmity to God? doubtless they are an abomination to him. What then, must not unregenerate men pray? I answer, it is their duty to breathe out holy desires to God in pray's. Prayer is a natural duty. Hannah pour'd out her soul before the Lord, yet her voice

was

was not heard, only her lips moved. Some grieve and complain that their pray's are not answered, but if *thy will be done is*, as it ought to be, in every prayer; their prayers are answer'd."

The wind was high at N. E. all day yesterday, but nothing fell from the dark clouds that overspread the heavens, till 8 o'clock last evening, when a snow began which has continued falling ever since. The bell being now ringing for 1 o'clock P. M. & no sign of abatement.

My aunt Deming says, that if my memory had been equal to the memory of some of my ancestors, I might have done better justice to Mr. Bacon's good sermon, & that if hers had been better than mine she would have helped me. Mr Bacon *did* say what is here recorded, but in other method.

April 6. — I made a shift to walk to meeting yesterday morning. But there was so much water in the streets when I came home from meeting that I got a seat in Mr Waleses chaise. My aunt walk'd home & she sais thro' more difaculty than ever she did in her life before. Indeed had the stream get

up

up from our meeting house as it did down, we might have taken boat as we have talk'd some times of doing to cross the street to our oposite neighbor *Soley's* chaise. I remember some of Mr Hunts sermon, how much will appear in my text journal.

April 7. — I visited yesterday P. M. with my aunt at Mr Waldron's. This afternoon I am going with my aunt to visit Mrs Salisbury who is Dr Sewall's granddaughter, I expect Miss Patty Waldow will meet me there. It is but a little way & we can now thro' favour cross the street without the help of a boat. I saw Miss Polly Vans this morning. She gives her love to you. As she always does whenever I see her. Aunt Deming is this minute come into the room, & from what her niece has wrote last, takes the liberty to remind you, that Miss Vans is a sister of the Old South Church, a society remarkable for Love. Aunt Deming is sorry she has spoil'd the look of this page by her carelessness & hopes her niece will mend its appearance in what follows. She wishes my English had been better, but has not time to correct more than one word.

April

April 9. — We made the visit refer'd to above. The company was old Mrs Salisbury,[60] Mrs Hill, (Mrs Salisbury's sister she was Miss Hannah Sewall & is married to young Mr James Hill that us'd to live in this house) Miss Sally Hill, Miss Polly Belcher Lyde, Miss Caty Sewall, My Aunt & myself. Yesterday afternoon I visited Miss Polly Deming & took her with me to Mr Rogers' in the evening where Mr Hunt discours'd upon the 7th question of the catechism viz what are the decrees of God? I remember a good many of his observations, which I have got set down on a loose paper. But my aunt says that a Miss of 12 year's old cant possibly do justice to the nicest subject in Divinity, & therefore had better not attempt a repetition of perticulars, that she finds lie (as may be easily concluded) somewhat confused in my young mind. She also says, that in her poor judgment, Mr Hunt discours'd soundly as well as ingeniously upon the subject, & very much to her instruction & satisfaction. My Papa inform'd me in his last letter that he had done me the honor to read my journals & that he

approv'd

approv'd of some part of them, I suppose he means that he likes some parts better than other, indeed it would be wonderful, as aunt says, if a gentleman of papa's understanding & judgment cou'd be highly entertain'd with *every little* saying or observation that came from a girl of my years & that I ought to esteem it a great favour that he notices any of my simple matter with his *approbation.*

April 13th. — Yesterday I walk'd to meeting all day, the ground very dry, & when I came home from meeting in the afternoon the Dust blew so that it almost put my eyes out. What a difference in the space of a week. I was just going out to writing school, but a slight rain prevented so aunt says I must make up by writing well at home. Since I have been writing the rain is turn'd to snow, which is now falling in a thick shower. I have now before me, hond Mamma, your favor dated January 3. I am glad you alter'd your mind when you at first thought not to write to me. I am glad my brother made an essay for a Post Script to your Letter. I must get him to read it to me, when he comes up, for two

reasons

reasons, the one is because I may have the pleasure of hearing his voice, the other because I don't understand his characters. I observe that he is mamma's "Ducky Darling." I never again shall believe that Mrs Huston will come up to Boston till I see her here. I shall be very glad to see Mrs Law here & I have some hopes of it. Mr Gannett and the things you sent by him we safely receiv'd before I got your Letter — you say "you see I am still a great housekeeper," I think more so than when I was with you. Truly I answer'd Mr Law's letter as soon as I found opportunity therefor. I shall be very glad to see Miss Jenny here & I wish she could live with me. I hope you will answer this "viva vosa" as you say you intend to. Pray mamma who larnt you lattan? It now rains fast, but the sun shines, & I am glad to see it, because if it continues I am going abroad with aunt this afternoon.

April 14th. — I went a visiting yesterday to Col. Gridley's with my aunt. After tea Miss Becky Gridley sung a minuet. Miss Polly Deming & I danced to her musick,

which

which when perform'd was approv'd of by
Mrs Gridley, Mrs Deming, Mrs Thompson,
Mrs Avery,[61] Miss Sally Hill, Miss Becky
Gridley, Miss Polly Gridley & Miss Sally
Winslow. Col[n] Gridley was out o' the room.
Col[n] brought in the talk of Whigs & Tories
& taught me the difference between them.
I spent last evening at home. I should have
gone a visiting to day in sudbury street, but
Unkle Harry told me last night that they
would be full of company. I had the pleasure of hearing by him, that they were all
well. I believe I shall go somewhere this
afternoon for I have acquaintances enough
that would be very glad to see me, as well
as my sudbury street friends.

April 15th. — Yesterday I din'd at Mrs.
Whitwell's & she being going abroad, I
spent the afternoon at Mad[m] Harris's & the
evening at home, Unkle Harry gave us his
company some part of it. I am going to
Aunt Storer's as soon as writing school is
done. I shall dine with her, if she is not
engaged. It is a long time since I was there,
& indeed it is a long time since I have been
able to get there. For tho' the walking has
been

been pretty tolerable at the South End, it has been intolerable down in town. And indeed till yesterday, it has been such bad walking, that I could not get there on my feet. If she had wanted much to have seen me, she might have sent either one of her chaises, her chariot, or her babyhutt,[62] one of which I see going by the door almost every day.

April 16th. — I dined with Aunt Storer yesterday & spent the afternoon very agreeably at Aunt Suky's. Aunt Storer is not very well, but she drank tea with us, & went down to Mr Stillman's lecture in the evening. I spent the evening with Unkle & Aunt at Mrs Rogers's. Mr Bacon preach'd his fourth sermon from Romans iv. 6. My cousin Charles Storer lent me Gulliver's Travels abreviated, which aunt says I may read for the sake of perfecting myself in reading a variety of composures. she sais farther that the piece was desin'd as a burlesque upon the times in which it was wrote, — & Martimas Scriblensis & Pope Dunciad were wrote with the same design & as parts of the same work, tho' wrote by three several hands.   April

April 17th. — You see, Mamma, I comply with your orders (or at least have done father's some time past) of writing in my journal every day tho' my matters are of little importance & I have nothing at present to communicate except that I spent yesterday afternoon & evening at Mr Soley's. The day was very rainy. I hope I shall at least learn to spell the word *yesterday*, it having occur'd so frequently in these pages! (The bell is ringing for good friday.) Last evening aunt had a letter from Unkle Pierce, he informs her, that last Lords day morning Mrs Martin was deliver'd of a daughter. She had been siezed the Monday before with a violent pluritick fever, which continued when my Unkle's letter was dated 13th instant. My Aunt Deming is affraid that poor Mrs Martin is no more. She hopes she is reconcil'd to her father — but is affraid whether that was so — She had try'd what was to be done that way on her late visits to Portsmouth, & found my unkle was placably dispos'd, poor Mrs Martin, she could not then be brought to make any acknowledgements as she ought to have done.

April

April 18th. — Some time since I exchang'd a piece of patchwork, which had been wrought in my leisure intervals, with Miss Peggy Phillips,[63] my schoolmate, for a pair of curious lace mitts with blue flaps which I shall send, with a yard of white ribbin edg'd with green to Miss Nancy Macky for a present. I had intended that the patchwork should have grown large enough to have cover'd a bed when that same live stock which you wrote me about some time since, should be increas'd to that portion you intend to bestow upon me, should a certain event take place. I have just now finish'd my Letter to Papa. I had wrote to my other correspondents at Cumberland, some time ago, all which with this I wish safe to your & their hand. I have been carefull not to repeat in my journal any thing that I had wrote in a Letter either to papa, you, &c. Else I should have inform'd you of some of Bet Smith's abominations with the deserv'd punishment she is soon to meet with. But I have wrote it to papa, so need not repeat. I guess when this reaches you, you will be too much engag'd in preparing to quit your
present

present habitation, & will have too much upon your head & hands, to pay much attention to this scrowl. But it may be an amusement to you on your voyage — therefore I send it.

Pray mamma, be so kind as to bring up all my journal with you. My Papa has promised me, he will bring up my baby house with him. I shall send you a droll figure of a young lady,[64] in or under, which you please, a tasty head Dress. It was taken from a print that came over in one of the last ships from London. After you have sufficiently amused yourself with it I am willing . . .

Boston April 20, 1772. — Last Saterday I seal'd up 45 pages of Journal for Cumberland. This is a very stormy day — no going to school. I am learning to knit lace.

April 21. — Visited at uncle Joshua Green's. I saw three funerals from their window, poor Cap^n Turner's was one.

April 22^d. — I spent this evening at Miss Rogers as usual. Mr. Hunt continued his discourse upon the 7th question of the catechism & finish'd what he had to say upon it.

April 23^d. — This morn^g early our Mr Bacon

con set out upon a tour to Maryland, he pro-
posed to be absent 8 weeks. He told the
Church that brother Hunt would supply the
pulpit till his return. I made a visit this
afternoon with cousin Sally at Dr. Phillip's.

April 24th. — I drank tea at Aunt Suky's.
Aunt Storer was there, she seemed to be in
charming good health & spirits. My cousin
Charles Green seems to grow a little fat
pritty boy but he is very light. My aunt
Storer lent me 3 of cousin Charles' books to
read, viz. — The puzzeling cap, the female
Oraters & the history of Gaffer too-shoes.[65]

April 25th. — I learn't three stitches upon
net work to-day.

April 27th. — I din'd at Aunt Storer's &
spent the P. M. at aunt Suky's.

April 28th. — This P. M. I am visited by
Miss Glover, Miss Draper & Miss Soley.
My aunt abroad.

April 29th. — Tomorrow, if the weather be
good, I am to set out for Marshfield.

May 11. — The morning after I wrote
above, I sat out for Marshfield. I had the
pleasure of drinking tea with aunt Thomas
the same day, the family all well, but Mr G

who

MRS. EBENEZER STORER

who seems to be near the end of the journey of life. I visited General Winslow [66] & his son, the Dr., spent 8 days very agreeably with my friends at Marshfield, & returned on saterday last in good health & gay spirits which I still enjoy. The 2 first days I was at Marshfield, the heat was extream & uncommon for the season. It ended on saterday evening with a great thunder storm. The air has been very cool ever since. My aunt Deming observ'd a great deal of lightning in the south, but there was neither thunder, rain nor clouds in Boston.

May 16. — Last Wednesday Bet Smith was set upon the gallows. She behav'd with great impudence. Thursday I danc'd a minuet & country dances at school, after which I drank tea with aunt Storer. To day I am somewhat out of sorts, a little sick at my stomach.

23^d. — I followed my schools every day this week, thursday I din'd at aunt Storer's & spent the P. M. there.

25. — I was not at meeting yesterday, Unkle & Aunt say they had very good Fish at the O. S. I have got very sore eyes.

June

June 1st. — All last week till saterday was very cold & rainy. Aunt Deming kept me within doors, there were no schools on account of the Election of Councellers,[67] & other public doings ; with one eye (for t'other was bound up) I saw the governer & his train of life guard &c. ride by in state to Cambridge. I form'd Letters last week to suit cousin Sally & aunt Thomas, but my eyes were so bad aunt would not let me coppy but one of them. Monday being Artillery Election[68] I went to see the hall, din'd at aunt Storer's, took a walk in the P. M. Unkle laid down the commission he took up last year. Mr Handcock invited the whole company into his house in the afternoon & treated them very genteelly & generously, with cake, wine, &c. There were 10 corn baskets of the feast (at the Hall) sent to the prison & almshouse.

4th. — From June 1 when I wrote last there has nothing extraordinary happen'd till today the whole regiment muster'd upon the common. Mr Gannett, aunt & myself went up into the common, & there saw Capt Water's, Capt Paddock's, Capt Peirce's, Capt Eliot's, Capt

Capt Barret's, Capt Gay's, Capt May's, Capt Borington's & Capt Stimpson's company's exercise. From there, we went into King street to Col Marshal's [69] where we saw all of them prettily exercise & fire. Mr. Gannett din'd with us. On Sabbath-day evening 7 June My Hon^d Papa, Mamma, little Brother, cousin H. D. Thomas, Miss Jenny Allen, & Mrs Huston arriv'd here from Cumberland, all in good health, to the great joy of all their friends, myself in particular — they sail'd from Cumberland the 1st instant, in the evening.

Aug. 18. — Many avocations have prevented my keeping my journal so exactly as heretofore, by which means a pleasant visit to the peacock, my Papa's & mamma's journey to Marshfield &c. have been omitted. The 6 instant Mr Saml Jarvis was married to Miss Suky Peirce, & on the 13th I made her a visit in company with mamma & many others. The bride was dress'd in a white satin night gound.[70]

27. — Yesterday I heard an account of a cat of 17 years old, that has just recovered of the meazels. This same cat it is said had the small pox 8 years ago! 28.

28. — I spent the P. M. & eve at aunt Suky's very agreeably with aunt Pierce's young ladies viz. Miss Johnson, Miss Walker, Miss Polly & Miss Betsey Warton, (of Newport) Miss Betsey is just a fortnight wanting 1 day older than I am, who I became acquainted with that P. M. Papa, Mamma, Unkle & aunt Storer, Aunt Pierce & Mr & Mrs Jarvis was there. There were 18 at supper besides a great many did not eat any. Mrs Jarvis sang after supper. My brother Johny has got over the measels.

Sept. 1. — Last evening after meeting, Mrs Bacon was brought to bed of a fine daughter. But was very ill. She had fits.

September 7. — Yesterday afternoon Mr Bacon baptiz'd his daughter by the name of Elizabeth Lewis. It is a pretty looking child. Mrs Whitwell is like to loose her Henry Harris. He is very ill.

8. — I visited with mamma at cousin Rogers'. There was a good many.

14. — Very busy all day, went into the common in the afternoon to see training. It was very prettyly perform'd.

18. — My Papa, aunt Deming, cousin Rogers,

&

& Miss Betsey Gould set out for Portsmouth.
I went over to Charlestown with them, after
they were gone, I came back, & rode up from
the ferry in Mrs Rogers' chaise ; it drop'd
me at Unkle Storer's gate, where I spent the
day. My brother was very sick.

Sep[r] 17. 18. — Spent the days at aunt
Storer's, the nights at home.

19. — Went down in the morn[g] & spent
the day & night there. My brother better
than he was.

20. — Sabbath day. I went to hear Mr
Stilman [71] all day, I like him very much. I
don't wonder so many go to hear him.

21st. — Mr. Sawyer, Mr Parks, & Mrs Chat-
bourn, din'd at aunt Storer's. I went to
dancing in the afternoon. Miss Winslow &
Miss Allen visited there.

22[d]. — The king's coronation day. In the
evening I went with mamma to Col[n] Marshal's in King Street to see the fireworks.

23[d]. — I din'd at aunt Suky's with Mr &
Mrs Hooper [72] of Marblehead. In the afternoon I went over to see Miss Betsy Winslow.
When I came back I had the pleasure to
meet papa. I came home in the evening to
see

see aunt Deming. Unkle Winslow sup'd
here.

24. — Papa cal'd here in the morn^g. Nothing else worth noticeing.

25. — Very pleasant. Unkle Ned cal'd
here. Little Henry Harris was buried this
afternoon.

26. 27. — Nothing extraordinary yesterday
& to day.

28. — My papa & unkle Winslow spent the
evening here.

29. 30. — Very stormy. Miss Winslow &
I read out the Generous Inconstant, & have
begun Sir Charles Grandison. . . .

May 25. — Nothing remarkable since the
preceding date. Whenever I have omited a
school my aunt has directed me to sit it down
here, so when you dont see a memorandum of
that kind, you may conclude that I have paid
my compliments to mess^{rs} Holbrook & Turner (to the former you see to very little purpose) & mrs Smith as usual. The Miss Waldow's I mentioned in a former are Mr. Danl
Waldo's daughters (very pretty misses) their
mamma was Miss Becca Salisbury.[73] After
making a short visit with my Aunt at Mrs
Green's

Green's, over the way, yesterday towards
evening, I took a walk with cousin Sally to
see the good folks in Sudbury Street, & found
them all well. I had my HEDDUS roll on,
aunt Storer said it ought to be made less,
Aunt Deming said it ought not to be made
at all. It makes my head itch, & ach, & burn
like anything Mamma. This famous roll is
not made *wholly* of a red *Cow Tail*, but is a
mixture of that, & horsehair (very course) &
a little human hair of yellow hue, that I suppose was taken out of the back part of an old
wig. But D—— made it (our head) all carded
together and twisted up. When it first came
home, aunt put it on, & my new cap on it,
she then took up her apron & mesur'd me,
& from the roots of my hair on my forehead
to the top of my notions, I mesur'd above an
inch longer than I did downwards from the
roots of my hair to the end of my chin.
Nothing renders a young person more amiable than virtue & modesty without the help
of fals hair, red *Cow tail*, or D—— (the bar-
ber).[74] Now all this mamma, I have just
been reading over to my aunt. She is pleas'd
with my whimsical description & grave (half

grave

grave) improvement, & hopes a little fals
English will not spoil the whole with Mamma.
Rome was not built in a day.

31st May. — Monday last I was at the factory to see a piece of cloth cousin Sally spun
for a summer coat for unkle.   After viewing
the work we recollected the room we sat down
in was Libberty Assembly Hall, otherwise
called factory hall, so Miss Gridley & I did ourselves the Honour of dancing a minuet in it.
On tuesday I made Mrs Smith my morning
& p. m. visits as usual, neither Mr. Holbrook
nor Turner have any school this week, nor
till tuesday next.   I spent yesterday with my
friends in sudbury St.   Cousin Frank has
got a fever, aunt Storer took an emmetick
while I was there, cousin Betsy had violent
pains almost all the forenoon.   Last tuesday
Miss Ursula Griswold, daughter of the right
Hon. Matthew Griswold Esq governer of one
of his Majesty's provinces, was made one of
our family, & I have the honor of being her
chambermade.   I have just been reading
over what I wrote to the company present, &
have got myself laughed at for my ignorance.
It seems I should have said the daughter of
                                        the

the Hon Lieu⁺. Governor of Connecticutt.
Mrs Dixon lodg'd at Capⁿ Mitchell's. She
is gone to Connecticutt long since.

31 May. — I spent the afternoon at unkle
Joshua's. yesterday, after tea I went to see
how aunt Storer did. I found her well at
Unkle Frank's. Mr Gerrish & wife of Halifax I had the pleasure to meet there, the latter sends love to you. Indeed Mamma, till
I receiv'd your last favour, I never heard a
word about the little basket &c. which I sent
to brother Johny last fall. I suppose Harry
had so much to write about cotton, that he
forgot what was of more consequence. Dear
Mamma, what name has Mr Bent given his
Son ? something like Nehemiah, or Jehosha-
phat, I suppose, it must be an odd name (our
head indeed, Mamma.) Aunt says she hopes
it a'nt Baal Gad, & she also says that I am
a little simpleton for making my note within
the brackets above, because, when I omit to
do it, Mamma will think I have the help of
somebody else's head but, N. B. for herself
she utterly disclames having either her head
or hand concern'd in this curious journal,
except where the writing makes it manifest.
So much for this matter.

CUT-PAPER PICTURE

NOTES.

Aunt Deming was Sarah, the oldest child of John Winslow and Sarah Peirce, and therefore sister of Joshua Winslow, Anna Green Winslow's father. She was born August 2, 1722, died March 10, 1788. She married John West, and after his death married, on February 27, 1752, John Deming. He was a respectable and intelligent Boston citizen, but not a wealthy man. He was an ensign in the Ancient and Honorable Artillery in 1771, and a deacon of the Old South Church in 1769, both of which offices were patents of nobility in provincial Boston. They lived in Central Court, leading out of Washington Street, just south of Summer Street. Aunt Deming eked out a limited income in a manner dear to Boston gentlewomen in those and in later days; she took young ladies to board while they attended Boston schools. Advertisements in colonial newspapers of "Board and half-board for young ladies" were not rare, and many good old New England names are seen in these advertisements. Aunt Deming was a woman of much judgment, as is shown in the pages of this diary; of much power of graphic description, as is
proved

proved by a short journal written for her niece, Sally Coverly, and letters of hers which are still preserved. She died childless.

NOTE 2.

Cumberland was the home in Nova Scotia of Anna Green Winslow's parents, where her father held the position of commissary to the British regiments stationed there. George Green, Anna's uncle, writing to Joseph Green, at Paramaribo, on July 23, 1770, said: "Mr. Winslow & wife still remain at Cumberland, have one son & one daughter, the last now at Boston for schooling, &c." So, at the date of the first entry in the diary, Anna had been in Boston probably about a year and a half.

NOTE 3.

Anna Green Winslow had doubtless heard much talk about this Rev. John Bacon, the new minister at the Old South Church, for much had been said about him in the weekly press: whether he should have an ordination dinner or not, and he did not; accounts of his ordination; and then notice of the sale of his sermons in the *Boston Gazette*.

All Mr. Bacon's parishioners did not share Anna's liking for him; he found himself at the Old South in sorely troubled waters. He made a most unpropitious and trying entrance at best, through succeeding the beloved Joseph Sewall, who had preached to Old South listeners for fifty-six years. He came to town a stranger. When, a month later, Governor Hutchinson

son issued his annual Thanksgiving Proclamation, there was placed therein an "exceptionable clause" that was very offensive to Boston patriots, relating to the continuance of civil and religious liberties. It had always been the custom to have the Proclamation read by the ministers in the Boston churches for the two Sundays previous to Thanksgiving Day, but the ruling governor very cannily managed to get two Boston clergymen to read his proclamation the third Sunday before the appointed day, when all the church members, being unsuspectingly present, had to listen to the unwelcome words. One of these clerical instruments of gubernatorial diplomacy and craft was John Bacon. Samuel Adams wrote bitterly of him, saying, "He performed this servile task a week before the time, when the people were not aware of it." The *Boston Gazette* of November 11 commented severely on Mr. Bacon's action, and many of his congregation were disgusted with him, and remained after the service to talk the Proclamation and their unfortunate new minister over.

It might have been offered, one might think, as some excuse, that he had so recently come from Maryland, and was probably unacquainted with the intenseness of Massachusetts politics ; and that he had also been a somewhat busy and preoccupied man during his six weeks' presence in Boston, for he had been marrying a wife, — or rather a widow. In the *Boston Evening Post* of November 11, 1771, I read this notice: " Married, the Rev'd John Bacon to Mrs. Elizabeth Cummings, daughter of Ezekiel Goldthwait, Esq." He

He retained his pastorate, however, in spite of his early mistake, through anxious tea-party excitement and forlorn war-threatened days, till 1775, with but scant popularity and slight happiness, with bitter differences of opinion with his people over atonement and imputation, and that ever-present stumbling-block to New England divines, — baptism under the Half Covenant, — till he was asked to resign.

Nor did he get on over smoothly with his fellow minister, John Hunt. In a curious poem of the day, called " Boston Ministers " (which is reprinted in the *New England Historical and Genealogical Register* of April, 1859), these verses appear : —

> At Old South there 's a jarring pair,
>   If I am not mistaken,
> One may descry with half an eye
>   That Hunt is far from Bacon.
> Wise Hunt can trace out means of grace
>   As leading to conversion,
> But Hopkins scheme is Bacons theme,
>   And strange is his assertion.

It mattered little, however, that Parson Bacon had to leave the Old South, for that was soon no longer a church, but a riding school for the British troops.

Mr. Bacon retired, after his dismissal, to Canterbury, Conn., his birthplace. His friendly intimacy with Mrs. Deming proved of value to her, for when she left Boston, in April, 1775, at the time of the closing of the city gates, she met Mr. Bacon in Providence. She says in her journal : —

" Towards

"Towards evening M^r & Mrs Bacon, with their
daughter, came into town. Mr Bacon came to see
me. Enquir'd into my designs, &c. I told him truely
I did not know what to do. That I had thot of
giting farther into the country. Of trying to place
Sally in some family where she might earn her board,
& to do something like it for Lucinda, or put her
out upon wages. That when I left the plain I had
some faint hope I might hear from Mr Deming while
I continued at Providence, but that I had little of
that hope remaining. Mr Bacon advised me to go
into Connecticutt, the very thing I was desirous of.
Mr Bacon sd that he would advise me for the present
to go to Canterbury, his native place. That he would
give me a Letter to his Sister, who would receive me
kindly & treat me tenderly, & that he would follow
me there in a few days."

This advice Mrs. Deming took, and made Canterbury her temporary home.

Mr. Bacon did not again take charge of a parish.
After the Revolution he became a magistrate, went
to the legislature, became judge of the court of common pleas, and a member of congress. He did not
wholly give up his disputatious ways, if we can judge
from the books written by and to him, one of the
latter being, "A Droll, a Deist, and a John Bacon,
Master of Arts, Gently Reprimanded."

His wife, who was born in 1733, and died in Stock-
bridge in 1821, was the daughter of Ezekiel Goldthwait, a Tory citizen of Boston, a register of deeds,
and a wealthy merchant. A portrait of Mrs. Bacon,
painted

painted by Copley, is remarkable for its brilliant eyes and beautiful hands and arms.

NOTE 4.

Rev. John Hunt was born in Northampton, November 20, 1744. He was a Harvard graduate in the class of 1764, a classmate of Caleb Strong and John Scollay. He was installed colleague-pastor of the Old South Church with John Bacon in 1771. He found it a most trying position. He was of an amiable and gentle disposition, and the poem on "Boston Ministers" asserted that he "most friends with sisters made." Another Boston rhymester called him "puny John from Northampton, a meek-mouth moderate man." When the gates of Boston were closed in 1775, after the battle of Lexington, he returned to Northampton, and died there of consumption, December 20, 1775. A full account of his life is given in *Sprague's Annals of the American Pulpit.* See also Note 3.

NOTE 5.

"Unkle and Aunt Winslow" were Mr. and Mrs. John Winslow. He was the brother of Joshua Winslow, was born March, 1725–26, died September 29, 1773, in Boston. He was married, on March 12, 1752, to Elizabeth Mason (born September, 1723, died January, 1780). They had five children: I. Gen. John Winslow, born September 26, 1753, married Ann Gardner, May 21, 1782, died November 29, 1819. II. Sarah, born April 12, 1755, married Deacon

con Samuel Coverly, of Boston, on November 27, 1787, died April 3, 1804. See Note 13. III. Henry, born January 11, 1757, died October 13, 1766. IV. Elizabeth, born November 28, 1759, died September 8, 1760. V. Elizabeth, born September 14, 1760, married John Holland, died November 21, 1795.

Gen. John Winslow was the favorite nephew of Joshua Winslow and of his wife, and largely inherited their property. He remained in Boston through the siege, and preserved the communion plate of the Old South Church by burying it in his uncle Mason's cellar. He was an ardent patriot, and it is said that his uncle Joshua threatened to hang him if he caught him during the Revolutionary War. The nephew answered, " No catchee — no hangee, Uncle ; " but did have the contrary fortune of capturing the uncle, whom he released on parole. He was the sixth signer and first treasurer of the Society of the Cincinnati. General Winslow's daughter, Mary Ann Winslow, born in 1790, lived till 1882, and from her were obtained many of the facts given in these notes.

NOTE 6.

Miss Soley was Hannah Soley, daughter of John Soley and Hannah Carey, who were married October 11, 1759. Hannah Soley was born June 5, 1762, and married W. G. McCarty.

NOTE 7.

William and Samuel Whitwell and their families were members of the Old South Church, and all were friends

friends of the Winslows and Demings. William Whitwell was born September 3, 1714, died April 10, 1795. He was a prosperous merchant, an estimable and useful citizen, and church member. His first wife was Rebecca Keayne, his second Elizabeth Scott (or Swett), who died May 13, 1771 ; his third, the widow of Royal Tyler. The Mrs. Whitwell here referred to must have been Mrs. Samuel Whitwell, for William Whitwell just at that interval was a widower. Samuel Whitwell was born December 17, O. S. 1717, died June 8, 1801. His first wife was Elizabeth Kelsey; his second, Sarah Wood ; his third, Mary Smith.

NOTE 8.

Polly Deming was a niece of John Deming.

NOTE 9.

Miss Polly Glover was Mary Glover, born in Boston, October 12, 1758, baptized at the Old South Church, married to Deacon James Morrell, of the Old South, on April 23, 1778, and died April 3, 1842. She was the daughter of Nathaniel Glover (who was born May 16, 1704, in Dorchester; died December, 1773), and his wife, Anne Simpson. They were married in 1750. Nathaniel Glover was a graduate of Harvard, and a wealthy man ; partner first of Thomas Hancock, and then of John Hancock.

NOTE 10.

Miss Bessy Winslow was Elizabeth, Anna's cousin, who was then about ten years old. See Note 5.

NOTE

NOTE 11.

Miss Nancy or Anne Glover was Mary Glover's sister. See Note 9. She was born in Boston, March 28, 1753, baptized in the Old South Church, died in Roxbury, August, 1797. She married Samuel Whitwell, Jr., son of Samuel Whitwell, a prominent Boston merchant. See Note 7.

NOTE 12.

Miss Sally Winslow was Sarah, daughter of John Winslow (see Note 5), and was, therefore, Anna's cousin. She was born April 12, 1755, died April 3, 1804. She married, November 27, 1787, Samuel Coverly, deacon of the Old South Church. She was the Sally Coverly for whom Mrs. Deming's journal was written. Several of Sally Coverly's letters still exist, and are models of elegant penmanship and correct spelling, and redound to the credit of her writing teacher, Master Holbrook. All the d's and y's and t's end with elaborately twisted little curls. A careful margin of an inch is left on every side. The letters speak so plainly of the formal honor and respect paid by all well-bred persons of the day to their elders, even though familiar kinsfolk, that I quote one, which contains much family news : —

BOSTON, Feb. 17th, 1780.

I thank you my dear Aunt for your kind Epistles of April 9th & Nov'r 10th, the kind interestedness you yet continue to take in my concerns merits the warmest returns of Gratitude.

The

The Particular circumstances you wish to know I shall with pleasure inform you of — Mr. Coverly is the youngest son of a Worthy Citizen late of this town but his Parents are now no more. His age is thirty-five. His Occupation a Shopkeeper who imports his own goods. And if you should wish to know who of your acquaintance he resembles, Madam, I would answer He has been taken for our Minister Mr Eckley, by whom we were married in my Aunt Demings sick chamber the 27th of Nov'r last twelve months since. He has two Brothers who both reside in town. I have been remarkably favor'd the last year as to my health & we are blest likewise with a fine little Daughter between 4 & 5 months old, very healthy, which we have named Elizabeth for its Grandmamas and an Aunt of each side. My Brother call'd today & inform'd me that Mr Powell intended setting out tomorrow for Quebeck & left a Letter for you which I shall send with this. He is almost if not quite as big as my uncle was last time I saw him — he was well & his family, he has three sons, the youngest about eleven months old, he has buried one.

In your last you mention both my Uncle & yourself as not enjoying so great a share of health. I hope by this time you have each regain'd that blessing more perfectly. Be pleased with him My Dear Aunt to accept My Duty in which Mr Coverly joins me.

My Sister was very well last week & her son John who is a fine child about 3 months old. Capt. Holland has purchas'd a house near fort hill which has

remov'd

remov'd her to a greater distance from me. She is now gone to the West-indies, she is connected in a family that are all very fond of her. We expect soon to remove. Mr Coverly has taken a lease of a house for some years belonging to Mr John Amory, you will please to direct your next for us in Cornhill N° 10, I shall have the pleasure of your friend Mrs Whitwell for my next neighbor there. I had not the pleasure of seeing Mr Freeman whiles here altho' I expected it, as his brother promis'd to wait on him here.

In one of your kind Epistles, Madam, you mention'd some of your Movables which you would wish me to take possession of which were at my Uncle Demings. The Memorandum you did not send me & my Uncle Deming has none nor knows of any thing but a great wheel.

He is now maried to the Widow Sebry who is very much lik'd and appears to be a Gentlewoman, they were very well today. My Aunt Mason was to see me a few weeks since with Mrs Coburn Mrs Scolly & Miss Becky Scolly from Middleborough. Mrs Scolly has since married her youngest daughter to Mr Prentice, Minister of Medfield.

Please to give my Love to Cousin Sally Deming if she is yet with you I hope she has regain'd her usual health. I should be very glad to be inform'd how her Mamma is & where & her family.

Be pleased to continue your Indulgence, as your
Epistles

Epistles My Dear Aunt will at all times be most gratefully receiv'd by

Y^r Oblidg'd Niece

SARAH COVERLY.

NOTE 13.

Josiah Waters, Jr., was the son of Josiah and Abigail Dawes Waters. The latter lived to be ninety-five years old. Josiah Sr. was a captain in the Artillery Company in 1769, and Josiah Jr. in 1791. The latter married, on March 14, 1771, Mary, daughter of William and Elizabeth Whitwell. See Note 7. Their child, Josiah Waters, tertius, born December 29, 1771, lived till August 4, 1818. He was a Latin School boy, and in the class with Josiah Quincy at Harvard.

NOTE 14.

The life of this slave-girl Lucinda was a fair example of the gentle form of slavery which existed till this century in our New England States. From an old paper written by a daughter of Gen. John Winslow, I quote her description of this girl : —

"Lucinda was born in Africa and purchased by Mrs Deming when she was about seven years of age. She was cherished with care and affection by the family, and at Mrs. Demings death was 'given her freedom.' From that time she chose to make her home with 'Master John' (the late Gen. John Winslow, of Boston), a nephew of Mrs Demings — at his house she died after some years. The friends

of

of the Winslow family attended her funeral ; her pastor the Rev Dr Eckley of the Old South and Gen. W. walking next the hearse as chief mourners. **A** few articles belonging to her are preserved in the family as memorials of one who was a beloved member of the household in the olden time."

Lucinda figures in Mrs. Deming's account of her escape from besieged Boston in 1775, and was treated with as much consideration as was Sally, the niece ; for her mistress remained behind for a time at Wrentham, rather than to allow Lucinda to ride outside the coach in the rain.

In a letter written by Sally Coverly, August 6, 1795, to Mrs. Joshua Winslow, at Quebec, she says : "You enquire about Lucinda, she is very much gratified by it. She has lived with my Brother this ten years and is very good help in their family."

NOTE 15.

The " Miss Sheafs " were Nancy and Mary Sheaffe, youngest daughters of William Sheaffe, who had recently died, leaving a family of four sons and six daughters. He had been deputy collector of customs under Joseph Harrison, the last royal collector of the port. He left his family penniless, and a small shop was stocked by friends for Mrs Sheaffe. I have often seen her advertisements in Boston newspapers.

Mrs. Sheaffe was Susanna Child, daughter of Thomas Child, an Englishman, one of the founders of Trinity Church. She lived till 1811. The ten children grew up to fill dignified positions in life.
One

One son was Sir Roger Hale Sheaffe. Susanna, at
the age of fifteen, made a most romantic runaway
match with an English officer, Capt. Ponsonby Moles-
worth. Margaret married John R. Livingstone ; she
was a great beauty. Lafayette, on his return to
France, sent her a satin cardinal lined with ermine,
and an elegant gown. Helen married James Lovell.
(See Note 52.) Nancy, or Anne Sheaffe, married, in
September, 1786, John Erving, Jr., a nephew of
Governor Shirley, and died young, leaving three children, — Maria, Frances, and Major John Erving.
Mary married Benj. Cutler, high sheriff of Boston,
and died December 8, 1784, leaving no children.
These Sheaffes were nearly all buried in the Child
tomb in Trinity Church.

NOTE 16.

Governor Matthew Griswold was born March 25,
1714, died April 28, 1799. He married, on Nov. 10,
1743, his second cousin, Ursula Wolcott, daughter of
Gov. Roger Wolcott. A very amusing story is told
of their courtship. Governor Griswold in early life
wished to marry a young lady in Durham, Conn.
She was in love with a physician, whom she hoped
would propose to her, and in the mean time was un-
willing to give up her hold upon her assured lover.
At last the governor, tired of being held in an uncer-
tainty, pressed her for a definite answer. She pleaded
that she wished for more time, when he rose with
dignity and answered her, " I will give you a life-
time." This experience made him extremely shy,
and

and when thrown with his cousin Ursula he made no advance towards love-making. At last when she was nineteen and he ten years older she began asking him on every occasion, "What did you say, Cousin Matthew?" and he would answer her quietly, "Nothing." At last she asked him impatiently, "What did you say, Cousin Matthew?" and when he answered again "Nothing," she replied sharply, "Well, it's time you did," — and *he did*.

Their daughter Ursula, the visitor at Mrs. Deming's, was born April 13, 1754, and was a great beauty. She married, in November 22, 1777, her third cousin, Lynde McCurdy, of Norwich, Conn.

Note 17.

"Unkle Joshua" was Joshua Green, born in Boston, May 17, 1731, "Monday ½ past 9 oclock in the morns" and died in Wendell, Mass., on September 2, 1811. He attended the Boston Latin School in 1738, and was in the class of 1749 at Harvard. He married, as did his brother and sister, a Storer — Hannah, daughter of Ebenezer and Mary Edwards Storer — on October 7, 1762. After his marriage he lived in Court Street, the third house south of Hanover Street. His wife Hannah was for many years before and after her marriage — as was her mother — the intimate friend and correspondent of Abigail Adams, wife of John Adams. Some of their letters may be found in the *Account of Percival and Ellen Green and Some of their Descendants*, written by Hon. Samuel Abbott Green, who is a great-grandson of Joshua and Hannah Green. Note

NOTE 18.

Madam Storer was Mary Edwards Storer, the widow of Ebenezer Storer, a Boston merchant. She was the mother of Anna's uncle Ebenezer Storer, of her aunt Hannah Storer Green, and of her aunt Mary Storer Green. See Notes 19, 32, 59.

NOTE 19.

Miss Caty Vans was the granddaughter of Hugh Vans, a merchant of Boston, who became a member of the Old South Church in 1728. He was born in Ayr, Scotland, in 1699. He married Mary Pemberton, daughter of Rev. Ebenezer Pemberton, and died in Boston in 1763. They had four sons, John, Ebenezer, Samuel, and William. One of the first three was the father of Caty Vans, who was born January 18, 1770. There are frequent references to her throughout the diary, but I know nothing of her life. William Vans married Mary Clarke, of Salem, and had one son, William, and one daughter, Rebecca, who married Captain Jonathan Carnes. The Vans family Bible is in the library of the Essex Institute.

NOTE 20.

In the cordial hatred of the Puritans for Christmas Anna heartily joined. It was not till this century that in New England cheerful merriment and the universal exchange of gifts marked the day as a real holiday.

NOTE

NOTE 21.

"Aunt Sukey" was Susanna Green, born July 26, 1744, died November 10, 1775. She married, on October 18, 1769, her cousin, Francis Green. The little child Charles, of whom Anna writes, proved to be a deaf-mute, and was drowned near Halifax in 1787. Francis Green had two deaf-mute children by a second wife, and became prominent afterwards in Massachusetts for his interest in and promotion of methods in instructing the deaf. In a letter of George Green's, dated Boston, July 23, 1770, we read: "Frank Green was married to Sukey in October last and they live next house to Mrs Storers." From another, dated December 5, 1770: "Frank keeps a ship going between here & London, but I believe understands little of the matter, having never been bred to business wch was one great objection with my father to his courting Sukey." I think he must have developed into a capable business man, for I have frequently seen his business advertisements in Boston newspapers of his day. Anna's mother bequeathed seven hundred and fifty dollars to Francis Green in her will. He was a man universally esteemed in the community.

NOTE 22.

Dr. Samuel Cooper was born March 28, 1725; died December 29, 1783. He graduated at Harvard in 1743, and became pastor of the Brattle Street Congregational Church, of Boston. He was a brilliant preacher, an ardent patriot, the intimate friend of John Adams and Benjamin Franklin, and a very handsome man.   NOTE

Note 23.

Master Holbrook was Samuel Holbrook, Anna's writing-master, one of a highly honored family of Boston writing teachers. Perhaps the best known of this family was Abiah Holbrook. In the *Boston Gazette* of January 30, 1769, I find this notice : —

" Last Friday morning died Mr Abiah Holbrook in the 51st year of his Age, Master of the South Writing School in this Town. He was looked upon by the Best Judges as the Greatest Master of the Pen we have ever had among us, of which he has left a most beautiful Demonstration. He was indefatigable in his labours, successful in his Instructions, an Honour to the Town and to crown all an Ornament to the Religion of Jesus. His Funeral is to be Attended Tomorrow Afternoon at Four Oclock."

The " beautiful Demonstration " of his penmanship which he left behind him was a most intricate piece of what was known as "fine knotting " or " knot work." It was written in " all the known hands of Great Britain." This work occupied every moment of what Abiah Holbrook called his "spare time " for seven years. It was valued at £100. It was bequeathed to Harvard College, unless his wife should need the money which could be obtained from selling it. If this were so, she was to offer it first for purchase to John Hancock. Abiah was a stanch patriot.

Samuel Holbrook was a brother of Abiah. He began teaching in 1745, when about eighteen years old. A petition of Abiah, dated March 10, 1745–46, sets forth that his school had two hundred and twenty scholars

scholars (Well may his funeral notice say that he was indefatigable in his labors !), that finding it impossible to properly instruct such a great number, he had appointed his brother to teach part of them and had paid his board for seven months, else some of the scholars must have been turned off without any instruction. He therefore prayed the town to grant him assistance. Think of one master for such a great school! In 1750 Samuel Holbrook's salary as usher of the South Writing School was fifty pounds per annum.

After serving as writing-master of the school in Queen Street, and also keeping a private school, he was chosen master of the South Writing School in March, 1769, to supply the place of his brother Abiah deceased. His salary was one hundred pounds. In 1776, and again in 1777, he received eighty pounds in addition to his salary. He also was a patriot. He was one of the " Sons of Liberty " who dined at the Liberty Tree, Dorchester, on August 14, 1769; and he was a member of Captain John Haskin's company in 1773. He was a member of the Old South Church, and he died July 24, 1784. In his later years he kept a school at West Street, where afterwards was Amos Lawrence's garden.

Abiah and Samuel left behind them better demonstrations of their capacity than pieces of " knotwork " — in the handwriting of their scholars. They taught what Jonathan Snelling described as " Boston Style of Writing," and loudly do the elegant letters and signatures of their scholars, Boston patriots,
clergy,

clergy, and statesmen, redound to the credit of the Masters Holbrook.

Other Holbrooks taught in Boston. From the Selectmen's Minutes of that little town, we find that on November 10, 1773, —

" Mr Holbrook, Master of the Writing School in the Common, and Mr Carter the Master Elect of the school in Queen St having recommended Mr Abiah Holbrook, a young man near of age, as a suitable person to be usher at Mr Carters school — the Selectmen sent for him, and upon discoursing with the young man thought proper to appoint him usher of said school."

And from the *Boston Gazette*, of April 17, 1769, we learn that Mr. Joseph Ward "Opened an English Grammar School in King St where Mr Joseph Holbrook hath for many years kept a Writing School."

These entries of Anna's relating to her attending Master Holbrook's school have an additional value in that they prove that both boys and girls attended these public writing schools, — a fact which has been disputed.

NOTE 24.

Dr. James M. Lloyd, born March 14, 1728, died March 14, 1810. He began his medical practice in 1752. He was appointed surgeon of the garrison at Boston, and was a close friend of Sir William Howe and Earl Percy, who for a time lived in his house. He was an Episcopalian, and one of the indignant protesters against the alteration of the liturgy at King's Chapel. Though a warm Tory and Loyalist,

he

he was never molested by the American government. He was one of Boston's most skilful and popular physicians for many years. While other city doctors got but a shilling and sixpence for their regular fee, he charged and received the exorbitant sum of half a dollar a visit; and for "bringing little master to town," in which function he was a specialist, he charged a guinea.

NOTE 25.

A pincushion was for many years, and indeed is still, in some parts of New England, a highly conventional gift to a mother with a young babe. Mrs. Deming must have made many of these cushions. One of her manufacture still exists. It is about five inches long and three inches wide; one side is of white silk stuck around the edge with old-fashioned clumsy pins, with the words, "John Winslow March 1783. Welcome Little Stranger." The other side is of gray satin with green spots, with a cluster of pins in the centre, and other pins winding around in a vine and forming a row round the edge.

NOTE 26.

Though the exchange of Christmas gifts was rare in New England, a certain observance of New Year's Day by gifts seems to have obtained. And we find in Judge Sewall's diary that he was greeted on New Year's morn with a levet, or blast of trumpets, under his window; and he celebrated the opening of the eighteenth century with a very poor poem of his own composition,

composition, which he caused to be recited through Boston streets by the town-crier.

NOTE 27.

The word "pompedore" or Pompadour was in constant use in that day. We read of pompedore shoes, laces, capes, aprons, sacques, stockings, and head-dresses.

NOTE 28.

Aunt Storer was Mrs. Ebenezer Storer. Her maiden name was Elizabeth Green. She was a sister of Mrs. Joshua Winslow. She was born October 12, 1734, died December 8, 1774; was married July 17, 1751, to Ebenezer Storer, who was born January 27, 1729–30, died January 6, 1807. He was a Harvard graduate, and was for many years treasurer of that college. He was one of Boston's most intellectual and respected citizens. His library was large. His name constantly appears on the lists of subscribers to new books. After his death his astronomical instruments became the property of Harvard College, and as late as 1843 his comet-finder was used there.

As Anna Green Winslow spent so much of her time in her "Aunt Storers" home in Sudbury Street, it is interesting to know that a very correct picture of this elegant Boston home of colonial days has been preserved through the account given in the *Memoir of Eliza Susan Morton Quincy*, — though many persons still living remember the house: —

"The mansion of Ebenezer Storer, an extensive edifice

edifice of wood three stories in height, was erected in
1700. It was situated on Sudbury Street between
two trees of great size and antiquity. An old English
elm of uncommon height and circumference grew in
the sidewalk of the street before the mansion, and
behind it was a sycamore tree of almost equal age
and dimensions. It fronted to the south with one
end toward the street. From the gate a broad walk
of red sandstone separated it from a grass-plot which
formed the courtyard, and passed the front door to
the office of Mr. Storer. The vestibule of the house,
from which a staircase ascended, opened on either
side into the dining and drawing rooms. Both had
windows towards the courtyard and also opened by
glazed doors into a garden behind the house. They
were long low apartments ; the walls wainscoted and
panelled ; the furniture of carved mahogany. The
ceilings were traversed through the length of the
rooms by a large beam cased and finished like the
walls ; and from the centre of each depended a glass
globe which reflected as in a convex mirror all sur-
rounding objects. There was a rich Persian carpet
in the drawing-room, the colors crimson and green.
The curtains and the cushions of the window-seat
were of green damask ; and oval mirrors and giran-
doles and a teaset of rich china completed the furniture of that apartment. The wide chimney-place in
the dining room was lined and ornamented with
Dutch tiles ; and on each side stood capacious arm-
chairs cushioned and covered with green damask, for
the master and mistress of the family. On the walls
were

were portraits in crayon by Copley, and valuable engravings representing Franklin with his lightning rod, Washington, and other eminent men of the last century. Between the windows hung a long mirror in a mahogany frame; and opposite the fireplace was a buffet ornamented with porcelain statuettes and a set of rich china. A large apartment in the second story was devoted to a valuable library, a philosophical apparatus, a collection of engravings, a solar microscope, a camera, etc."

As I read this description I seem to see the figure of our happy little diary-writer reflected in the great glass globes that hung from the summer-trees, while she danced on the Persian carpet, or sat curled up reading on the cushioned window-seat.

Note 29.

As this was in the time of depreciated currency, £45 was not so large a sum to spend for a young girl's outfit as would at first sight appear.

Note 30.

Dr. Charles Chauncey was born January 1, 1705; died February 10, 1787. He graduated at Harvard in 1721, and soon became pastor of the First Church in Boston. He was an equally active opponent of Whitefield and of Episcopacy. He was an ardent and romantic patriot, yet so plain in his ways and views that he wished *Paradise Lost* might be turned into prose that he might understand it.

Note

NOTE 31.

Rev. Ebenezer Pemberton was pastor of the New Brick Church. He had a congregation of stanch Whigs; but unluckily, the Tory Governor Hutchinson also attended his church. Dr. Pemberton was the other minister of the two who sprung the Governor's hated Thanksgiving proclamation of 1771 on their parishes a week ahead of time, as told in Note 3, and the astounded and disgusted New Brick hearers, more violent than the Old South attendants, walked out of meeting while it was being read. Dr. Pemberton's troubled and unhappy pastorate came to an end by the closing of his church in war times in 1775. He was of the 1721 class of Harvard College. He died September 9, 1777.

NOTE 32.

We find frequent references in the writings and newspapers of the times to this truly Puritanical dread of bishops. To the descendants of the Pilgrims the very name smacked of incense, stole, and monkish jargon. A writer, signing himself "America," gives in the *Boston Evening Post*, of October 14, 1771, a communication thoroughly characteristic of the spirit of the community against the establishment of bishops, the persistent determination to "beate down every sprout of episcopacie."

NOTE 33.

A negligée was a loose gown or sacque open in front, to be worn over a handsome petticoat; and in spite

spite of its name, was not only in high fashion for many years, but was worn for full dress. Abigail Adams, writing to Mrs. Storer, on January 20, 1785, says: " Trimming is reserved for full dress only, when very large hoops and negligées with trains three yards long are worn." I find advertised in the *Boston Evening Post*, as early as November, 1755: " Horse-hair Quilted Coats to wear with Negligees." A poem printed in New York in 1756 has these lines: —

> " Put on her a Shepherdee
> A Short Sack or Negligee
> Ruffled high to keep her warm
> Eight or ten about an arm."

NOTE 34.

A pistoreen was a Spanish coin worth about seventeen cents.

NOTE 35.

There exists in New England a tradition of "groaning cake," made and baked in honor of a mother and babe. These cakes which Anna bought of the nurse may have been "groaning cakes." It was always customary at that time to give "vails" to the nurse when visiting a new-born child; sometimes gifts of money, often of trinkets and articles of clothing.

NOTE 36.

Miss " Scolley " was Mary Scollay, youngest of the thirteen children of John Scollay (who was born in

1712, died October, 1799), and his wife Mary. Mary was born in 1759. She married Rev. Thomas Prentiss on February 9, 1798, had nine children, and lived to be eighty-two years old — dying in 1841. Her sister Mercy was engaged to be married to General Warren, but he fell at Bunker Hill: and his betrothed devoted herself afterwards to the care and education of his orphaned children whom he had by his first wife.

NOTE 37.

Miss Bella Coffin was probably Isabella, daughter of John Coffin and Isabella Child, who were married in 1750. She married Major MacMurde, and their sons were officers in India.

NOTE 38.

This Miss "Quinsey" was Ann Quincy, the daughter of Col. Josiah Quincy (who was born 1710, died 1784), and his third wife, Ann Marsh. Ann was born December 8, 1763, and thus would have been in her ninth year at the time of the little rout. She married the Rev. Asa Packard, of Marlborough, Mass., in 1790.

NOTE 39.

In the universal use of wines and strong liquors in New England at that date children took unrestrainedly their proportionate part. It seems strange to think of this girl assembly of little Bostonians drinking wine and hot or cold punch as part of their
"treat,"

"treat," yet no doubt they were well accustomed to such fare. I know of a little girl of still tenderer years who was sent at that same time from the Barbadoes to her grandmother's house in Boston to be "finished" in Boston schools, as was Anna, and who left her relative's abode in high dudgeon because she was not permitted to have wine at her meals; and her parents upheld her, saying Missy must be treated like a lady and have all the wine she wished. Cobbett, who thought liquor drinking the national disease of America, said that "at all hours of the day little boys at or under twelve years of age go into stores and tip off their drams." Thus it does not seem strange for little maids also to drink at a party. The temperance awakening of this century came none too soon.

Note 40.

Paste ornaments were universally worn by both men and women, as well as by little girls, and formed the decoration of much of the headgear of fashionable dames. Many advertisements appear in New England newspapers, which show how large and varied was the importation of hair ornaments at that date. We find advertised in the *Boston Evening Post*, of 1768: "Double and single row knotted Paste Combs, Paste Hair Sprigs & Pins all prices. Marcasite and Pearl Hair Sprigs, Garnet & Pearl Hair Sprigs." In the *Salem Gazette* and various Boston papers I read of "black & coloured plumes & feathers." Other hair ornaments advertised in the
Boston

Boston News Letter, of December, 1768, were "Long and small Tail Garnets, Mock Garland of all sorts and Ladies Poll Combs." Steel plumes, pompons, aigrettes, and rosettes all were worn on the head, and artificial flowers, wreaths of gauze, and silk ribbons.

NOTE 41.

Marcasite, spelled also marcassite, marchasite, marquesett, or marquaset, was a mineral, the crystallized form of iron pyrites. It was largely used in the eighteenth century for various ornamental purposes, chiefly in the decoration of the person. It took a good polish, and when cut in facets like a rose-diamond, formed a pretty material for shoe and knee-buckles, earrings, rings, pins, and hair ornaments. Scarce a single advertisement of wares of milliner or mantua maker can he found in eighteenth century newspapers that does not contain in some form of spelling the word marcasite, and scarce a rich gown or headdress was seen without some ornament of marcasite.

NOTE 42.

Master Turner was William Turner, a fashionable dancing master of Boston, who afterward resided in Salem, and married Judith, daughter of Dr. Edward Augustus Holyoke, of Salem, who died in 1829, aged one hundred and one years. It was recalled by an old lady that the scholars in the school of her youth marched through Boston streets, to the music of the fiddle played by " Black Henry," to Concert Hall,
corner

corner Tremont and Bromfield streets, to practice dancing; and that Mr. Turner walked at the head of the school. His advertisements may be seen in Boston and Salem papers, thus: —

"Mr. Turner informs the Ladies and Gentlemen in Town and Country that he has reduced his price for teaching from Six Dollars Entrance to One Guinea, and from Four Dollars per month to Three. Those ladies and Gentlemen who propose sending their children to be taught will notice no books will be kept as Mr. T. has suffered much by Booking. The pupils must pay monthly if they are desirous the School should continue."

NOTE 43.

"Unkle Ned" was Edward Green, born September 18, 1733; died July 29, 1790. He married, on April 14, 1757, Mary Storer (sister of Ebenezer Storer and of Hannah Storer Green). They had no children. He was, in 1780, one of the enlisting officers for Suffolk County. In a letter of George Green's, written July 25, 1770, we read: "Ned still lives gentlemanlike at Southwacks Court without doing any business tho' obliged to haul in his horns;" and from another of December 5, 1770: "Ned after having shown off as long as he cou'd with his yello damask window curtains &c is (the last month) retired into the country and lives wth his wife at Parson Storers at Watertown. How long that will hold I cant say."

NOTE

Note 44.

Madam Smith was evidently Anna's teacher in sewing. The duties pertaining to a sewing school were, in those days, no light matter. From an advertisement of one I learn that there were taught at these schools : —

"All kinds of Needleworks viz : point, Brussels, Dresden Gold, Silver, and silk Embroidery of every kind. Tambour Feather, India & Darning, Spriggings with a Variety of Open-work to each. Tapestry plain, lined, and drawn. Catgut, black & white, with a number of beautiful Stitches. Diaper and Plain Darnings. French Quiltings, Knitting, Various Sorts of marking with the Embellishments of Royal cross, Plain cross, Queen, Irish, and Tent Stitches."

Can any nineteenth century woman read this list of feminine accomplishments without looking abashed upon her idle hands, and ceasing to wonder at the delicate heirlooms of lace and embroidery that have come down to us !

Note 45.

Grandmamma Sargent was Joshua Winslow's mother. Her maiden name was Sarah Pierce. She was born April 30, 1697, died August 2, 1771. She married on September 21, 1721, John Winslow, who lived to be thirty-eight years old. After his death she married Dr. Nathaniel Sargent in 1749.

NOTE

Note 46.

These lines were a part of the epitaph said to be composed by Governor Thomas Dudley, who died at Andover, Mass., in 1653. They were found after his death and preserved in Morton's *New England's Memorial.* They run thus: —

> Dim eyes, deaf ears, cold stomach show
> My dissolution is in view;
> Eleven times seven near lived have I,
> And now God calls, I willing die;
> My shuttle's shot, my race is run,
> My sun is set, my deed is done;
> My span is measur'd, tale is told,
> My flower is faded and grown old,
> My dream is vanish'd, shadow's fled,
> My soul with Christ, my body dead;
> Farewell dear wife, children and friends,
> Hate heresy, make blessed ends;
> Bear poverty, live with good men,
> So shall we meet with joy again.
> Let men of God in courts and churches watch
> O'er such as do a toleration hatch;
> Lest that ill egg bring forth a cockatrice,
> To prison all with heresy and vice.
> If men be left, and other wise combine
> My epitaph's, I dy'd no libertine.

Note 47.

Miss Polly Vans was Mary Vans, daughter of Hugh and Mary Pemberton Vans, and aunt of Caty Vans. She was born in 1733. We have some scattered glimpses of her life. She joined the Old South

in

in 1755. In the *Boston Gazette*, of April 9, 1770, we read, "Fan Mounts mounted by Mary Vans at the house of Deacon Williams, in Cornhill." We hear of her at Attleborough with Samuel Whitwell's wife when the gates of Boston were closed, and we know she married Deacon Jonathan Mason on Sunday evening, December 20, 1778. She was his second wife. His first wife was Miriam Clark, and was probably the Mrs. Mason who was present at Mrs. Whitwell's, and died June 5, 1774. Mary Vans Mason lived till 1820, having witnessed the termination of eight of the pastorates of the Old South Church. Well might Anna term her "a Sister of the Old South." She was in 1817 the President of the Old South Charity School, and is described as a "disinterested friend, a judicious adviser, an affectionate counsellor, a mild but faithful reprover, a humble, self-denying, fervent, active, cheerful Christian." Jonathan Mason was not only a deacon, but a prosperous merchant and citizen. He helped to found the first bank in New England. His son was United States Senator. Two other daughters of Hugh Vans were a Mrs. Langdon, of Wiscasset, Maine, and Mrs. John Coburn.

NOTE 48.

St. Valentine's Day was one of the few English holidays observed in New England. We find even Governor Winthrop writing to his wife about "challenging a valentine." In England at that date, and for a century previous, the first person of the opposite

site

site sex seen in the morning was the observer's valentine. We find Madam Pepys lying in bed for a long time one St. Valentine's morning with eyes tightly closed, lest she see one of the painters who was gilding her new mantelpiece, and be forced to have him for her valentine. Anna means, doubtless, that the first person she chanced to see that morning was "an old country plow-joger."

NOTE 49.

Boston was at that date pervaded by the spirit of Liberty. Sons of Liberty held meetings every day and every night. Daughters of Liberty held spinning and weaving bees, and gathered in bands pledging themselves to drink no tea till the obnoxious revenue act was repealed. Young unmarried girls joined in an association with the proud declaration, "We, the daughters of those Patriots who have appeared for the public interest, do now with pleasure engage with them in denying ourselves the drinking of foreign tea." Even the children felt the thrill of revolt and joined in patriotic demonstrations — and a year or two later the entire graduating class at Harvard, to encourage home manufactures, took their degrees in homespun.

NOTE 50.

The cut-paper pictures referred to are the ones which are reproduced in this book, and which are still preserved. Anna's father finally received them. Mrs. Deming and other members of the Winslow family

family seem to have excelled in this art, and are remembered as usually bringing paper and scissors when at a tea-drinking, and assiduously cutting these pictures with great skill and swiftness and with apparently but slight attention to the work. This form of decorative art was very fashionable in colonial days, and was taught under the ambitious title of Papyrotamia.

NOTE 51.

The "biziness of making flowers" was a thriving one in Boston. We read frequently in newspapers of the day such notices as that of Anne Dacray, of Pudding Lane, in the *Boston Evening Post*, of 1769, who advertises that she "makes and sells Head-flowers: Ladies may be supplied with single buds for trimming Stomachers or sticking in the Hair." Advertisements of teachers in the art of flower-making also are frequent. I note one from the *Boston Gazette*, of October 19, 1767: —

"To the young Ladies of Boston. Elizabeth Courtney as several Ladies has signified of having a desire to learn that most ingenious art of Painting on Gauze & Catgut, proposes to open a School, and that her business may be a public good, designs to teach the making of all sorts of French Trimmings, Flowers, and Feather Muffs and Tippets. And as these Arts above mentioned (the Flowers excepted) are entirely unknown on the Continent, she flatters herself to meet with all due encouragement; and more so, as every Lady may have a power of serving herself

herself of what she is now obliged to send to England for, as the whole process is attended with little or no expence. The Conditions are Five Dollars at entrance ; to be confin'd to no particular hours or time : And if they apply Constant may be Compleat in six weeks. And when she has fifty subscribers school will be opened, &c, &c."

NOTE 52.

This was James Lovell, the famous Boston schoolmaster, orator, and patriot. He was born in Boston October 31, 1737. He graduated at Harvard in 1756, then became a Latin School usher. He married Miss Helen Sheaffe, older sister of the "two Miss Sheafs" named herein; and their daughter married Henry Loring, of Brookline. He was a famous patriot: he delivered the oration in 1771 commemorative of the Boston Massacre. He was imprisoned by the British as a spy on the evidence of letters found on General Warren's dead body after the battle of Bunker Hill. He died in Windham, Maine, July 14, 1814. A full account of his life and writings is given in Loring's *Hundred Boston Orators.*

NOTE 53.

Nothing seems more revolting to our modern notions of decency than the inhuman custom of punishing criminals in the open streets. From the earliest days of the colonies the greatest publicity was given to the crime, to its punishment, and to the criminal. Anna shows, in her acquaintance with the vices of

Bet

Bet Smith, a painful familiarity with evil unknown in any well-bred child of to-day. Samuel Breck wrote thus of the Boston of 1771 : —

" The large whipping-post painted red stood conspicuously and prominently in the most public street in the town. It was placed in State Street directly under the windows of a great writing school which I frequented, and from them the scholars were indulged in the spectacle of all kinds of punishment suited to harden their hearts and brutalize their feelings. Here women were taken in a huge cage, in which they were dragged on wheels from prison, and tied to the post with bare backs on which thirty or forty lashes were bestowed among the screams of the culprit and the uproar of the mob. A little further in the street was to be seen the pillory with three or four fellows fastened by the head and hands, and standing for an hour in that helpless posture, exposed to gross and cruel jeers from the multitude, who pelted them incessantly with rotten eggs and every repulsive kind of garbage that could be collected."

There was a pillory in State Street in Boston as late as 1803, and men stood in it for the crime of sinking a vessel at sea and defrauding the underwriters. In 1771 the pillory was in constant use in Newport.

NOTE 54.

In 1770 British troops were quartered in Boston, to the intense annoyance and indignation of Boston inhabitants. Disturbances between citizens and soldiers were frequent, and many quarrels arose. On the

the night of March 5 in that year the disturbance became so great that the troops, at that time under command of Captain Preston, fired upon the unarmed citizens in King (now State) street, causing the death of Crispus Attucks, a colored man, Samuel Gray and James Caldwell, who died on the spot, and mortally wounding Patrick Carr and Samuel Maverick. At the burial of these slaughtered men the greatest concourse ever known in the colonies flocked to the grave in the Granary Burying Ground. All traffic ceased. The stores and manufactories were closed. The bells were tolled in all the neighboring towns.

Daniel Webster said, that from the moment the blood of these men stained the pavements of Boston streets, we may date the severance of the colony from the British empire.

The citizens demanded the removal of the troops, and the request was complied with. For many years the anniversary of this day was a solemn holiday in Boston, and religious and patriotic services were publicly held.

NOTE 55.

Mathew Byles was born March 15, 1707; died July 5, 1788. He was ordained pastor of the Hollis Street Congregational Church, of Boston, in 1733. He was a staunch Loyalist till the end of his days, as were his daughters, who lived till 1837. His chief fame does not rest on his name as a clergyman or an author, but as an inveterate and unmerciful jester.

NOTE

NOTE 56.

Henry Green, the brother of Anna's mother, was born June 2, 1738. He was a Latin School boy, was in business in Nova Scotia, and died in 1774.

NOTE 57.

This stove was a foot-stove, — a small metal box, usually of sheet tin or iron, enclosed in a wooden frame or standing on little legs, and with a handle or bail for comfortable carriage. In it were placed hot coals from a glowing wood fire, and from it came a welcome warmth to make endurable the freezing floors of the otherwise unwarmed meeting-house. Foot-stoves were much used in the Old South. In the records of the church, under date of January 16, 1771, may be read : —

" Whereas, danger is apprehended from the stoves that are frequently left in the meeting-house after the publick worship is over; Voted that the Saxton make diligent search on the Lords Day evening and in the evening after a Lecture, to see if any stoves are left in the house, and that if he find any there he take them to his house; and it is expected that the owners of such stoves make reasonable satisfaction to the Saxton for his trouble before they take them away."

The Old South did not have a stove set in the church for heating till 1783.

NOTE 58.

The first anniversary of the Boston Massacre was celebrated throughout the city, and a mass-meeting was

was held at the Old South Church, where James Lovell made a stirring address. See Notes 52 and 54.

NOTE 59.

The Queen's night-cap was a very large full cap with plaited ruffles, which is made familiar to us through the portraits of Martha Washington.

NOTE 60.

"Old Mrs. Sallisbury" was Mrs. Nicholas Salisbury, who was married in 1729, and was mother of Rebecca Salisbury, who became Mrs. Daniel Waldo, and of Samuel Salisbury, who married Elizabeth Sewall. See Note 73.

NOTE 61.

Mrs. John Avery. Her husband was Secretary of the Commonwealth and nephew of John Deming, who in his will left his house to John Avery, Jr.

NOTE 62.

A baby hutt was a booby-hutch, a clumsy, ill-contrived covered carriage. The word is still used in some parts of England, and a curious survival of it in New England is the word booby-hut applied to a hooded sleigh; and booby to the body of a hackney coach set on runners. Mr. Howells uses the word booby in the latter signification, and it may be heard frequently in eastern Massachusetts, particularly in Boston.

NOTE

NOTE 63.

Peggy Phillips was Margaret Phillips, daughter of William and Margaret Wendell Phillips. She was born May 26, 1762, married Judge Samuel Cooper, and died February 19, 1844. She was aunt of Wendell Phillips.

NOTE 64.

This " droll figure " may have been a drawing, or a dressed doll, or " baby," as such were called — a doll that displayed in careful miniature the reigning modes of the English court. In the *New England Weekly Journal*, of July 2, 1733, appears this notice : —

" To be seen at Mrs. Hannah Teatts Mantua Maker at the Head of Summer Street Boston a Baby drest after the Newest Fashion of Mantuas and Night Gowns & everything belonging to a dress. Latily arrived on Capt. White from London, any Ladies that desire it may either come or send, she will be ready to wait on 'em if they come to the House it is Five Shilling, & if she waits on 'em it is Seven Shilling."

These models of fashion were employed until this century.

NOTE 65.

We can have a very exact notion of the books imported and printed for and read by children at that time, from the advertisements in the papers. In the *Boston Gazette and Country Journal*, of January 20, 1772, the booksellers, Cox and Berry, have this notice : —

The

The following Little Books for the Instruction & Amusement of all good Boys and Girls.

The Brother Gift or the Naughty Girl Reformed.

The Sister Gift, or the Naughty Boy Reformed.

Hobby Horse or Christian Companion.

Robin Good-Fellow, A Fairy Tale.

Puzzling Cap, A Collection of Riddles.

The Cries of London as exhibited in the Streets.

Royal Guide or Early Introduction to Reading English.

Mr Winloves Collection of Stories.

"   "   Moral Lectures.

History of Tom Jones	abridg'd from the works of
" " Joseph Andrews	H. Fielding.
" " Pamela	abridg'd from the works of
" " Grandison	S. Richardson, Esq.
" " Clarissa	

NOTE 66.

General John Winslow was but a distant kinsman of Anna's, for he was descended from Edward Winslow. He was born May 27, 1702 ; died April 17, 1774. He was a soldier and jurist, but his most prominent position (though now of painful notoriety) was as commander of that tragic disgrace in American history, the expedition against the Acadians. It is told in extenuation of his action that before the annihilation and dispersion of that unfortunate community he addressed them, saying that his duty was " very disagreeable to his natural make and temper as it must be grievous to them," but that he must obey orders, — and of course what he said was true.

NOTE

NOTE 67.

The exercises attending this election of counsellors must indeed have been an impressive sight. The Governor, attended by a troop of horse, rode from the Province House to Cambridge, where religious services were held. An Election Sermon was preached. Volleys and salutes were fired at the Battery and Castle. A protest was made in the public press, as on the previous year, against holding this election in Cambridge instead of in the "Town House in Boston, the accustomed Ancient Place," and also directly to the Governor, which was answered by him in the newspapers; and at this election a most significant event occurred — John Hancock declined to accept a seat among the counsellors, to which he had been elected. The newspapers — the *Massachusetts Spy* and the *Boston Gazette and Country Journal* — commented on his action thus : —

"Mr Hancocks declining a seat in the Council Board is very satisfactory to the Friends of Liberty among his constituents. This Gentleman has stood five years successively and as often Negativ'd. Whatever may have been the Motive of his being approbated at last his own Determination now shows that he had rather be a Representative of the People since he has had so repeatedly their Election and Confidence."

NOTE 68.

Boston had two election days. On Artillery Election the Ancient and Honorable Artillery had a dress parade

parade on the Common. The new officers were chosen and received their new commissions from the new Governor. No negroes were then allowed on the Common. The other day was called "Nigger Lection," because the blacks were permitted to throng the Common and buy gingerbread and drink beer, as did their betters at Artillery Election.

Note 69.

Col. Thomas Marshall was a Revolutionary officer. He commanded the Tenth Massachusetts Regiment at Valley Forge. He was Captain of the Ancient and Honorable Artillery from 1763 to 1767, and at one time commanded Castle Island, now Fort Independence. He was one of the Selectmen of Boston at the time when the town was invested by troops under Washington. He died at Weston, Mass., on November 18, 1800.

Note 70.

A night gown was not in those days a garment for wear when sleeping, but resembled what we now call a tea-gown. The night attire was called a rail. Both men and women wore in public loose robes which they called night gowns. Men often wore these gowns in their offices.

Note 71.

Many Boston people agreed with Anna in her estimate of Rev. Samuel Stillman. He was called to the First Baptist Church in 1765, and soon became one

of

of Boston's most popular and sensational preachers. Crowds thronged his obscure little church at the North End, and he took an active part in Revolutionary politics. Many were pleased with his patriotism who did not agree with him in doctrine. In the curious poem on Boston Ministers, already quoted, we read: —

> Last in my list is a Baptist,
> A real saint, I wot.
> Though named Stillman much noise he can
> Make when in pulpit got.
> The multitude, both grave and rude,
> As drove by wind and tide,
> After him hie, when he doth try
> To gain them to his side.

NOTE 72.

Mr. and Mrs. Hooper were "King" Hooper and his wife of Marblehead. He was so called on account of his magnificent style of living. He was one of the Harvard Class of 1763; was a refugee in 1775, and died insolvent in 1790. The beautiful mansion which he built at Danvers, Mass., is still standing in perfect condition, and is the home of Francis Peabody, Esq. It is one of the finest examples of eighteenth century architecture in New England.

NOTE 73.

This "Miss Becca" was Rebecca Salisbury, born April 7, 1731, died September 25, 1811. She was a fine, high-spirited young woman, and upon being taunted by a rejected lover with,

"The

> " The proverb old — you know it well,
> 　That women dying maids, lead apes in hell,"

(a belief referred to in *Taming of the Shrew*, Act II.
Scene 1), she made this clever rhyming answer : —

> " Lead apes in hell — tis no such thing ;
> 　The story's told to fool us.
> But better there to hold a string,
> 　Than here let monkeys lead us."

She married Daniel Waldo May 3, 1757. The
" very pretty Misses " were their daughters ; Elizabeth, born November 24, 1765, died unmarried in
Worcester, August 28, 1845 ; and Martha (who in
this diary is called Patty), born September 14, 1761,
died November 25, 1828. She married Levi Lincoln,
Lieutenant-Governor of Massachusetts, and became
the mother of Levi Lincoln, Governor of Massachusetts, Enoch Lincoln, Governor of Maine, and Col.
John Lincoln.

NOTE 74.

The fashion of the roll was of much importance
in those days. A roll frequently weighed fourteen
ounces. We can well believe such a heavy mass made
poor Anna's head " ach and itch like anything."
That same year the *Boston Gazette* had a laughable
account of an accident to a young woman on Boston
streets. She was knocked down by a runaway, and
her headdress received the most serious damage.
The outer covering of hair was thrust aside, and cotton, tow, and false hair were disgorged to the delight
of

of jeering boys, who kicked the various stuffings around the street. A Salem hair-dresser advertised that he would " attend to the polite construction of rolls to raise ladies heads to any pitch desired." The Abbé Robin, traveling through Boston a few years later, found the hair of ladies' heads " raised and supported upon rolls to an extravagant height."